The Road East to India

The Road East to India

Diary of a Journey of a Lifetime

Devika. A. Rosamund

Copyright © 2017 Devika A. Rosamund

The moral right of the author has been asserted.

Apart from any fair dealing for the purposes of research or private study, or criticism or review, as permitted under the Copyright, Designs and Patents Act 1988, this publication may only be reproduced, stored or transmitted, in any form or by any means, with the prior permission in writing of the publishers, or in the case of reprographic reproduction in accordance with the terms of licences issued by the Copyright Licensing Agency. Enquiries concerning reproduction outside those terms should be sent to the publishers.

Matador
9 Priory Business Park,
Wistow Road, Kibworth Beauchamp,
Leicestershire. LE8 0RX
Tel: 0116 279 2299
Email: books@troubador.co.uk
Web: www.troubador.co.uk/matador
Twitter: @matadorbooks

ISBN 978 1785898 716

British Library Cataloguing in Publication Data.
A catalogue record for this book is available from the British Library.

Printed and bound by CPI Group (UK) Ltd, Croydon, CR0 4YY
Typeset in 11pt Aldine401 BT by Troubador Publishing Ltd, Leicester, UK

Matador is an imprint of Troubador Publishing Ltd

Dedicated to all those of an adventurous spirit who are ready to risk everything to go into the unknown.

"India has been for centuries the symbol of the inner journey. It is not just a political entity – it is a spiritual phenomenon. As far back as we know, people have been coming to India from all over the world in search of themselves. Something is in the very climate, something is in the very vibe, that helps."

The Rebellious Spirit, Ch 15, by Osho

Contents

Preface		ix
Ch. 1	First Stop – Amsterdam	1
Ch. 2	On the 'Magic Bus' to India	19
	Athens, Greece	19
	Istanbul, Turkey	22
	Tehran, Iran	25
Ch. 3	Adventures in Afghanistan	32
Ch. 4	Travelling through Pakistan	47
	The Swat Valley in the Mountains	50
Ch. 5	India at Last	57
	Amritsar – Home of the Golden Temple	57
	Agra – Home of the Taj Mahal	62
Ch. 6	Varanasi – a Holy City	72
Ch. 7	The Majestic Himalayas and Tibetans	83
Ch. 8	Calcutta – Bedbugs and Poverty	91
Ch. 9	Puri and Hindu Temples	107
Ch.10	Sri Lanka – Island of Serendipity	120
	A Hut on the Beach	123
	More Island Adventures	129
Ch.11	A Boat Ride through Kerala and on to Goa	138
	Goa in the Monsoon	146
Ch.12	An Ashram in Pune	155
Ch.13	Meditation and a Therapy Group	170
Ch.14	Monsoon Floods and Inner Treasures	179

Preface

This is the authentic diary that I wrote in 1975 and 1976 as a twenty-two-year-old girl travelling alone overland from England to India. I started my journey in Amsterdam – where I worked for a few months – and there boarded the famous 'Magic Bus', as it was called in that era. I travelled as far as Iran on the bus and then continued my journey alone on local transport through Afghanistan and Pakistan until I reached India. I travelled all around India.

Nowadays it is sadly not possible to travel this route overland through so many countries anymore, because of the many political upheavals and disputes in the last thirty-five years. In those days it was the dream of many young travellers to make this journey overland and many of us were students. I went through these countries to make friends with the people, not to make war, as so many governments did afterwards. Everywhere I went, with very few exceptions, I was treated with friendliness and kindness by the local people.

My journey was also a spiritual quest, as it was for many of the people that I met on my travels. I am publishing my diary with the hope that it will inspire others to go on a journey both inner and outer, and explore this beautiful world and also their own world within.

Chapter One
First Stop – Amsterdam

Kent, England
Thursday, 7th August 1975

Ever since I was eleven years old I have known that I am going to travel to India and that I am going to find something there – something that will enrich my soul. I don't know what it is yet.

Recently I saw a television documentary about a place in Amsterdam in Holland called 'Cosmos' where yoga and meditation are taught. I am going to go to Amsterdam, work in any job I can find, and try to learn yoga and meditation in the evenings. There is a bus that goes regularly overland to India from Amsterdam. It takes six weeks to get there and journeys through many countries. It is famously called the 'Magic Bus'! If I manage to save enough money in Amsterdam, perhaps by next spring, I plan to get on that bus and go on my journey of a lifetime.

I have just finished a year of teaching in a primary school in the south of England. It was my first year of teaching after college. I loved the job and the children, but now I yearn for adventure. Now I want to travel the world and be free and experience new things. I want to live every day spontaneously and see what life brings to me.

The other night while I was lying in bed, I felt as though my spirit broke free from my body and touched the heights of Heaven. I was filled with a limitless peace and joy and love of all beings. It was so wonderful. I sat up in bed and looked in the dark at my body to see if I was still alive. I thought perhaps I had died and gone to Heaven! If Heaven is like that then I think I should never, ever be afraid to die. I shall not be afraid to travel the world no matter how dangerous it might seem.

Tomorrow I am going to enquire about the ferry that takes passengers over to Holland. I'm going to start the journey soon.

Amsterdam, Holland
Sunday, 7th September 1975

Yesterday I got off the boat and now I am here in the heart of Amsterdam. I can hardly believe it. A friend of mine called Pat who shared a house with me and some others when I was teaching, decided to come with me. We just checked into the first place we found when we arrived in this city. It is a rather crummy hostel — however it is a place to sleep! I have decided I don't want to travel like a wealthy tourist. It is much more of an adventure to travel cheaply and take what comes from day to day.

I went to the Van Gogh museum with a girl we met in the English Pub last night. Pat went with Jim to see a houseboat which we might rent on one of the canals. Jim is an Irishman we met on the boat from England to Vlissingen. We made friends with some other people coming across on the boat too. We have all been out looking for jobs.

First Stop - Amsterdam

Wednesday, 17th September 1975

I am feeling more settled now that I have been here for a while. We have moved into the big youth hostel in the centre of town. It is much nicer than the other hostel where we stayed at first. We are still waiting for the chance to move into the houseboat – that will be fun.

Each day feels like a fresh, open page ready for me to write on as I please. I feel more free than I have ever felt, yet I realise that it was only my state of mind when I felt tied down before. Life is always like an empty book that we can write on as we please if only we realise it.

I have obtained a job as a chambermaid at the Marriot Hotel in the centre of Amsterdam, and the hostel where we are staying is just around the corner. I want to do ordinary jobs now. My whole life has been just school and college, and then school again as a teacher. It is wonderful to let it all go for a while and take any job that comes my way. I want to have new experiences.

I am meeting so many people from different countries every day, both working in the hotel and staying in the hostel. Amsterdam is very international. None of the maids are Dutch – there are girls from Australia, Sweden, Poland, Italy and Portugal. It is a lot of fun but quite hard work.

I was thinking of staying here for a few weeks and then travelling on somewhere else for a while – perhaps to the south of France to pick grapes. There is an advert for that in the hostel. There is a yearning inside of me to keep on travelling. However, my friend Pat wants to stay here longer. At least we are earning good money here – almost twice as much as I was earning as a qualified teacher in England – the wages are so much higher here on the continent these days!

Pat and I had a couple of days off work and travelled north to the Dutch islands and visited Edam, Van Helder and Texel. Most of the way we hitch-hiked and met some interesting people. We stayed in the most beautiful house in Edam right by the canal. The houses look like dolls' houses – all shapes and sizes.

Saturday, 20th September 1975

I am sitting in Vondel Park which is close by our youth hostel. It is a beautiful park with many trees and is very peaceful here. Amsterdam is such a beautiful city but I wanted to be amongst nature so I decided to come for a walk after work. I don't want to write much – just to look at the beauty in the nature around me.

Tuesday, 23rd September 1975

This week we had two days off work again and went to Madurodam, the miniature model village which is near The Hague. It is beautiful, and shows important and picturesque buildings in Holland. We also went around the porcelain factory in Delft and saw a demonstration of the painting of the china. This is something I have always desired to do and I enquired about working there but they have no vacancies at the moment. However, we were told that we could do an apprenticeship there for six months if we liked. I would enjoy doing that but I am too restless to stay here for that long. I want to carry on travelling.

First Stop - Amsterdam

Wednesday, 24th September 1975

I love the numerous windmills that we see on our journeys around Holland. The canals in Amsterdam are full of houseboats and the buildings next to the canals are very picturesque. The houses there are tall and narrow and many of them were built in the 1600's. Amsterdam is such a small city that you can almost walk from one end to the other. I like it so much better than London.

Wednesday, 15th October 1975

The weather is getting colder. It even snowed on Monday morning. It was my day off and I was waiting in the queue to go on a tour of a brewery in Amsterdam with a group of friends from the hostel, Canadians and Australians. It was a strange experience to see snow in October. I enjoyed going to the brewery in spite of the cold wait. After a short tour of it we were led into a hall with tables and everyone sat around and drank beer – as much as they could drink in an hour! It was quite good fun and everyone was very merry afterwards. I had three beers and felt quite drunk as I am not used to drinking beer at all. I could barely walk home straight afterwards!

Sunday, 19th October 1975

I have now the best room in the hostel! Manfred, one of the wardens in the hostel reserved a two bedded room for Pat and me. He left red roses for me in the room with a note asking me out for dinner.

Wednesday, 22nd October 1975

This is a fairy-tale world – or so I felt yesterday as I wandered through the trees in Vondel Park again, amongst the autumn colours in the early morning. How beautiful it looks with the leaves changing colour all around me and lying like a carpet spread out upon the grass. So many delicate, feathery leaves like patterns around my feet and above my head as I looked up into the branches. I sat in meditation and gazed at the trees.

All the patterns of the leaves of each tree are the same; all of the same design, so perfectly symmetrical and yet not too perfect – that is what makes them so beautiful, I think, because they are the same and yet still all different. Each one is unique, as though they were cut out with nail scissors from the same pattern by someone who was not compulsive or obsessive – who did not worry if one leaf was slightly more pointed or more rounded than another. Neurotic exactness is not a characteristic of nature, of the mind of God – that is the perfection of it.

Friday, 24th October 1975

The other evening I had an interesting conversation with a Canadian guy at the bar about the 'Mind Dynamics' course he went on, and also about meditation because he saw that I was reading a book about meditation – *The Inner Reality* by Dr. Paul Brunton. I always bring my books down to the bar with me to read. I read an article recently which quoted a paragraph from a book called *The Shoes of the Fisherman* by Morris West. The quotation is very beautiful – I am going to paraphrase it here:

Morris West says that it costs so much to be a whole

human being that only very few have the enlightenment or the courage to pay the price. He says one has to abandon utterly the search for security. One has to be prepared to risk, and embrace life and the world with both arms like a lover. One has to be prepared to accept pain as a condition of existence and be open to doubt and darkness as the cost of knowing.

I love the idea of embracing life like a lover and abandoning the search for security. It does take courage to live life like that.

One of the books I am reading at the moment is 'The Primal Scream' by Arthur Janov Ph.D. which is about releasing repressed memories from childhood. It is very interesting.

I am writing this while waiting in the police station to have my passport stamped with a work permit. I have been waiting for ages! This morning I arrived at work late and my rooms had been given to someone else. They seemed to have too many staff today, and the housekeeper was having a problem finding everybody work, so I offered to take the day off. It is a good opportunity to come here and get my passport stamped.

Wednesday, 12th November 1975

I have found out where the 'Cosmos' centre is. That is the place I saw in the documentary on television that drew me here. Today I went up there and painted a picture. Cosmos is a lovely place – a meditation centre with an art room, library, yoga and meditation classes, and lectures especially associated with mystical subjects. I like the type of people who go there. I would like to start learning yoga and meditation soon.

Saturday, 15th November 1975

Last night I went to Cosmos again and joined the Vipassana meditation class. I have never done Vipassana meditation before. It was wonderful. I felt that my mind became very still and when I came out of the class I felt silent, and everything in the world looked more vibrant – colours were brighter and I was more aware of everything around me. Usually my mind is so full of thoughts, but I was free of them for a while.

I have made friends with a Portuguese girl called Lenny (short for Helene), who works with me as a chambermaid in the hotel. She is going to leave the hotel soon and go and work in a vegetarian macrobiotic restaurant called 'Mother's Milk' which is run by two American artists who are identical male twins. She is also brilliant at art and writes the most beautiful poetry in English. (She once studied in England.) I love talking to her because we have the same idealistic views about life – she is interested in mystical subjects like me. We go to Cosmos together to the yoga and meditation classes.

Lenny and I have both agreed that we would like to go to India on the 'Magic Bus' in the spring. We are both longing to travel east.

Saturday, 22nd November 1975

I was invited by the meditation teacher at Cosmos, who is called Bruno Martens, to go and stay for a few days in a communal village that is being built on an island down in the south of Holland. I went on the spur of the moment, but I am so glad I did for it was such a wonderful experience. It is a Buddhist community. They are vegetarians as I am, and live very frugally, working and living in the spirit of meditation. They practise Vipassana meditation every day. Every morning they go swimming in the freezing cold sea – I went with them and it was an exhilarating experience. I found the sea water warmer than the air outside!

I loved meditating with them every day on the island. We also did some construction work in the open air. I never really understood before what benefits can be derived from meditation, but now I have discovered it for myself. It is positively a healing process, especially beneficial for anybody suffering from stress.

I have found, in practising meditation with these Buddhists, that meditation empties the mind so that all there is left is a clear, clean, weightless space, and I feel freed from tension, weariness and worry. In meditation, my thoughts no longer envelop and overcome me like a fog, and for a while I can have a distance from them. I think that a mind tortured by too many thoughts is mental illness.

In Vipassana meditation, when we see thoughts within us, we observe them, like a movie being watched by someone else; we do not judge them or criticise them. As soon as we become aware of them they disappear, as a dream disappears in the morning. Meditation is like deep, dreamless sleep – it makes one feel calm but also very awake.

Now I am going to pack up my things and take them to the houseboat. Finally we are going to move in. Lenny and I will be sharing the houseboat with other friends.

Thursday 27th November 1975

I have now lived in the houseboat on the canal in Amsterdam for nearly a week. It takes quite a bit of getting used to! It is damp but we have two gas fires so it is not too cold.

The houseboat consists of three rooms; one is a sitting room and kitchen combined. We have a little gas stove and a sink with cold water – until the tank on the roof runs empty. It has to be filled with a hose from the furniture shop opposite. The hose has a hole in it so it is quite a job. Bill, one of the guys sharing the boat with us, usually fills the tank. Lenny and I sleep in the sitting room on a double mattress – it is warmer like that! Our blankets are sleeping bags unzipped and an old blanket we found here. I wear thick socks in bed and a jumper on top of my night dress! There is a little ladder down into the second room. Bill sleeps there on another mattress. In the third room are two other guys – one Scottish and one South African. Both are nice – we went out with them a few times for drinks.

The boat is not very clean inside. We sweep and shake the carpets, but everything is in a sad state of disrepair.

Now the summer season has finished we are no longer needed at the hotel and all this week I have been doing the rounds of the agencies trying to get work. At last I have found myself a temporary job in a nut factory – I start on Monday. It should be an experience anyway!

Saturday, 6th December 1975

I have worked four days in the nut factory now, packing nuts into boxes. It is very tedious and the hours are long, but there are other young people working here too and we are allowed to eat as many nuts as we like. We laugh together in the breaks and that makes it bearable.

I realise now that this is a strange existence for me – so different from my secure and respectable teaching job last year!

I am living a 'hippy-like' existence now, but this insecurity is more exciting, more spontaneous than my life before. I have given up that safe security in order to move into the unknown and travel the world and find myself and discover some truth within myself about my own being and about existence.

However, because I am trying to save money for my trip to India I feel as though I am not really living for the present moment any more, as I intended to do here. I am looking forward towards the future, doing jobs I don't really like. I wonder, is it right to sacrifice the present moment for something one wants in the future? I had decided before that it was not.

Friday, 12th December 1975

The other night on the houseboat I had a strange dream. It was quite beautiful. I saw the world in my dream as a huge brown rubber ball, not quite blown up. I was searching all over it.

In the dream, a voice spoke to me, and asked me: "What are you searching for?" I replied, "I am searching for the hole in the top of the world, because I know that when I have found it, I will be able to penetrate to the centre of the earth and from there I will be able to fly to the ends of the universe."

The voice said to me, "There is no need to search for this centre – it is possible to fly to the ends of the universe from the surface of the world." I pondered on this but decided to go on searching anyway, so I said to the voice, "I know that, but I just want to try anyway to see if there is a place."

Eventually, after what seemed like many days in the dream, suddenly, unexpectedly, I found the place and penetrated to the centre of the Earth. I was very surprised and overjoyed because

I did not really know whether such a place would exist. Then the dream ended with music like at the end of a film.

I know that this dream was influenced by my reading about meditation and my search for myself which is deep within me. I want my life to be such a quest. Nothing else is important to me. I know that if I could reach to this deepest inner part of me, my real self, then I would experience limitless freedom — hence the idea that I could soar to the utmost edges of the universe, of space.

At the yoga class I met an American guy who is training to be a yoga teacher. He told me he had lived a luxurious, extravagant life in America, but because he had never found happiness or fulfilment, he had come away to seek for it and discovered that happiness can only be found within oneself. He said he had found what he sought for in yoga. He advised me; "Give up the struggle, the fight against life. Let go and flow with the river of life." What he said touched me deeply.

I wish I could, I pray I could.

I am sitting in the library at Cosmos writing this. The books here are so interesting and the room has such a cosy, peaceful atmosphere.

I want to go on and on learning and discovering all my life. There must be no end, no point in time when I shall say, 'Now I have nothing more to learn.' Everything and every experience in life has to be a learning process.

Amsterdam is really beautiful now with lights and decorations in the streets and a big Christmas tree in the Dam Square. I wandered around the shops today. I love all the little souvenirs: especially the miniature paintings, blue Delft pottery, musical boxes and model windmills. I have bought a musical china windmill for my parents for a Christmas gift. I shall visit them at Christmas.

First Stop - Amsterdam

Tuesday, 16th December 1975

Lenny spends a lot of time in the vegetarian restaurant where she is now working as a macrobiotic cook. The people that go there are interesting and unconventional. She is lucky to have such a job. The food is wonderful – all health foods – and I often go there to sit and eat, and drink herb tea. I like to chat to the other people who go in there and read their books, or sit and read my own – or write when I want to express my thoughts.

One day when I was in the restaurant I saw a book called *My Way, The Way of the White Clouds* by a spiritual Master called Osho* in India. It is a book of his discourses which he gives daily in Pune*, India. The discourses are about the Tao, which means 'The Way'. There is a picture of the Master in the book – a wonderful-looking man with a long beard. I read the introduction in which someone has written, 'Christ is alive and well in Pune.' Of course, it cannot really be Christ, but perhaps someone like him. I read some of the words of his discourses in the book and was very impressed. He is saying: 'Be like a white cloud floating in the sky – it goes wherever the wind carries it.' This he says is Taoism: to be natural, and float or flow with the river of life – as my yoga friend said – to not fight with life or nature; to be grateful for whatever life brings to us, and to live in a state of let-go, in great trust. I love this philosophy. It fits with my desire to wander the Earth; to float like a white cloud wherever the wind takes me!

As I was looking at the book, one of the American twins – (Lenny's friends who own the restaurant) – saw me reading it and came up and said: "This is the man I would like to see."

Gary and Jerry, the twins, are tall, majestic-looking men with long hair and beards. They are artists and spiritual seekers who spend their nights painting and reading spiritual books. I have heard them say that we are in the Age of Aquarius and that something tremendous is going to happen on the planet. They seem to know so much about spiritual things that even though I have studied comparative religion and philosophy as subjects at college, I feel so incredibly ignorant in their presence. Often in the evenings when I come to the restaurant, I hear them talking about higher states of consciousness and spiritual energy (ideas I know little about) and I sit silently and listen. They seem so wise and I would like to pick up little bits of knowledge from them.

I have written down the name and address of the spiritual Master, Osho, in the back of my notebook. When I am in India I will perhaps go and visit him and see for myself. I have heard that there are 'godmen' in India – enlightened people – and I would love to meet one.

1976

Monday, 19th January 1976

I am working at Amsterdam airport, Schiphol, as a waitress. The agencies give us different jobs each week, but today I have a day off.

1975 has passed. I've opened a new page, begun a new chapter of my life with this new year.

My friend, an old school friend called Janette, has come across to Amsterdam to spend a month's holiday with me here. She has come to stay in our new rented flat in the centre of Amsterdam. We left the houseboat because it was becoming too cold to stay there. The water even froze in our tank on the roof!

Janette wants to go out and socialise and I have been going out with her to bars and discos. One night we went to a club and danced until 4.30 in the morning! We also went to a place called 'Melkweg'– I have been wanting to go there for ages. It is similar to Cosmos but a bit more freaky. Some people smoke marijuana in Amsterdam but as I don't smoke tobacco I would not know how to inhale it. I don't want to take drugs, but I did try a hashish cake there. It did not seem to have any effect on me but I am not going to try it again.

Janette met a Dutch guy and went out with him yesterday while I was at work. I want Janette to enjoy it here, but I was living such a purist life before – doing yoga and meditation. I think perhaps deep down I want to go out too and have some fun and live a bit more wildly – to experience this other side of life here. I think it is a tonic for me; at least, I think this is what I need at the moment.

Tuesday, 20th January 1976

Now I feel that there is an inner conflict in me. It is almost as if there are two parts of myself that want to be developed, acknowledged by me. Both parts are struggling, yearning to grow, to take me over. I am afraid that in giving way to one, I shall lose the other, and I am afraid that one is so elusive and ethereal that I can never touch it no matter how hard I try, while the other is so tangible, so easy, so obviously exciting – but it could never really quench that deeper spiritual thirst within me. Two paths lie open to me – one is spiritual and the other is worldly. I am sure of that and I want to try them both. Is it possible to tread those two opposite paths – if not at the same time, then can I try them separately?

One of the books that have influenced me the most in my life, (I read it last year) is 'Narziss and Goldmund' by Hermann Hesse. Those two men were both searching for the meaning of life, but one spent his life meditating in a monastery and the other one wandered the Earth in order to learn how to weather life's storms, to experience joy and pain and suffering, and know life in all its fullness – he also had many love affairs. They both searched for truth in different ways. This is my dilemma – which path to take to find truth, to find peace of spirit, to reach to the centre of my being? Is there not a way to travel on both paths, to experience both?

Wednesday, 28th January 1976

I know that there is a state, like another dimension, of tranquillity and beauty and inner peace that exists. Sometimes I have touched it; sometimes I have strayed into that kingdom – I felt that I did on Monday when I was out walking in Vondel Park. It was snowing soft, large gentle flakes all around me. The sky was filled with a heavenly twilight, so peaceful and beautiful. It was like a blessing from above, an offering of peace. It was like a communication with a higher realm. I would like to be able to communicate with that higher realm all of the time. I have heard that yogis who meditate can do this.

Thursday, 12th February 1976

Janette is going back to England soon. She says she has enjoyed it very much here – I am glad she has. My other friend Pat has also gone back to her own country, New Zealand.

I have decided now that I can't wait any longer to go to India! I am longing to board the Magic Bus – the 'famous' or 'infamous' bus that travels regularly overland from Amsterdam to India. Even if I don't have as much money as I would have liked (I will probably have only about £300 altogether) I don't care. I went to the office to enquire about buying a ticket for the bus. It takes six weeks altogether and stops on the way for several days in major cities to pick up other passengers. The ticket costs £60 one way, but I need extra money for food and accommodation for the six weeks' journey. Of course, I will stay in the cheapest of places, but that will be the fun of it. I don't want to travel like a rich tourist; as I said before, I want to experience life at its rawest. I expect that I will need about £100 to get to India and £100 to return on the bus. That will leave me with £100 to travel around India with. I'll carry it all in cash, English money, with my passport in a large zipped cloth shoulder bag I've made myself. I'll bring a rucksack with as few clothes as possible, a sleeping bag, and books to read on the journey as well as this journal I'm writing, of course!

I got a pleasant surprise when I arrived at the office and was shown photographs of very modern, comfortable-looking buses. I had imagined that the bus would be like the rusty old one painted with freaky pictures that I have seen parked in a street in Amsterdam. Most other people have also seen and heard about buses like that too – but I was told that the new buses they now have running are not like that anymore. Also, I was told that very few of them break down, contrary to popular belief. Everybody has heard stories of buses breaking down somewhere in the remote desert or lonely Himalayas!

Lenny has fallen in love with the twins who own the restaurant, so she has decided not to come with me on the bus at this time after all. She says she will come on a later bus with one of the twins – she is not sure which!

I have now waited so long to go to India that I simply cannot put it off any more. I have been working all these months. Recently I had a temporary job in an icy cold factory making blinds and lampshades. This winter is so freezing cold and I long to get away and start the journey that has been my dream for my whole life. Now I will go, and I have no fear of going alone. I love travelling alone.

Monday, 1st March 1976

I have now bought my ticket for the Magic Bus for next week! I went back to the office to buy it, and the girl behind the desk, before giving me the ticket, proceeded to warn me: "India is not the paradise that people think it is." She gave me a detailed description of a pile of huge insects she had seen swept into a corner of Delhi Airport and other airports while she was there! She has never been on the Magic Bus but once travelled to India by plane and did a two-week tour of that country, also by plane! She also told me about somebody who flew to India, saw the airport, and turned around and came straight back!

I am a bit squeamish where insects are concerned but if something like that would put me off, then God help me, I would not last long on my travels. I hope I have more guts than that!

I have never imagined that travelling is going to be a bowl of cherries; I have never imagined that India is going to be a bed of roses! I know there will be difficulties and dangers and adventures on the way and that I will be stretched to my limits.

Chapter Two

On the 'Magic Bus' to India

Athens, Greece
Wednesday, 10th March 1976

We are in Athens! The bus has stopped here for a few days to pick up passengers after travelling for three days and nights without stopping. There are two drivers and they take it in turns to drive. We have already travelled through Belgium, Germany, Austria and Yugoslavia.

It's a long time since I walked out in warm sunshine. For a couple of days before I left Amsterdam the sun shone weakly, giving us cheerful signs of spring at last, after such a long, cold and cheerless winter. I have never seen spring in Amsterdam, but those two sunny days in early March leave me with a preconception of what must be the beauty of spring days in that lovely city. There were flower markets and fruit markets opening everywhere. The canals sparkled in the sunlight, and buds showing green upon the trees gave promise of blossoms. I wandered through Vondel Park again before I left.

Now I am in Athens I remember Amsterdam with affection. Athens is a big, dusty, noisy city. It has its beauty spots, one of them being the area around the Acropolis and the 'Placa' (old part) with its flea market (where I am sitting now), quite Eastern in its wares, embroidered dresses and tunics, leather goods and Greek coffee pots, etc. The set-up of the town is familiar to me. I have been here before, and the memory of the streets, and even the Greek letters, comes back to me, like the gradual recollection of a faded dream. It is the atmosphere which is instinctively familiar to me – and the smells! And the cloudless sky. However, I feel uneasy here and even bored. I want to get away. We are leaving tomorrow afternoon.

My emotions on this trip are erratic. I felt no real sense of adventure actually until we entered Greece. I was busy observing the other passengers with interest. The few English people – so English (!) straight out of the mother country and London, two days ago! I felt quite proud of the feeling that I had at least been living in Holland. I was very conscious of hearing their English accents – one not very pleasant London accent which seemed to be a drawl of its own, all too familiar, as strong as any American accent I've heard. Even the Danes sitting in front of me – there are eight on the bus – expressed their dislike of the 'screeching voice', and, when I asked, assured me mine was not like that!

I discovered, though not until we had been travelling for twenty-four hours, that there is a boy from the city of Bath sitting opposite me on the bus. He left school a year or so ago and is now waiting to go to university. I like talking to him. I feel easy with him. I am going to study at Bath Teacher's Training College next year to complete my Bachelor of Education degree course. I am studying Comparative Religion and Philosophy as my main subjects.

I thought that the drivers were both English – but now I have discovered that the main driver (or boss!) is actually Icelandic. He seems to have a strong (but fairly nice) English accent and an English sense of humour. He is an ex-teacher and an obvious one at that! He talks to us passengers like school children (for fun, I suppose), and is the type of person that makes me feel annihilated in his presence, probably because he is such a very forceful, witty character. He has so much smug self-confidence that I don't feel easy with him. He treats me like a privileged passenger because I am a woman alone, buys me coffee, and kisses me on the lips in front of the other passengers every time he passes. I suppose I should feel flattered, but such strong people frighten me. I don't know what to reply to his quick, witty questions and comments. He sleeps on the back seat of the bus while the other driver is at the wheel during half the night.

He invited me to sleep there with him. I ended up doing it! After trying to sleep cold and upright on my own seat for a few hours one night, I gave in to my weaker feelings and went to the back with Barry! Anybody who has ever slept upright in a cramped position on a coach seat for two nights will know why, and the nights were so cold. It was warm and comfortable lying full out on the back seat (with all my clothes on of course), first with Barry, and then the other driver when he came to lie down next to me at three o'clock in the morning! It was completely innocent and certainly I had two good nights' sleep like that! I probably got myself a reputation with the other passengers. One of them asked me how long I had been working for the Sunshine Line. They thought I was working with the drivers! Now I've told everyone I am travelling alone, and people seem quite impressed. However, quite a lot of the men are travelling alone.

Barry invited me to stay in his hotel with him instead of the hostel when the bus stopped here in Athens to pick up passengers. The other driver invited me to share his room free with him too! I decided to refuse both offers, but then I found that there were no beds left in the hostel and I had to sleep on a cold marble floor. I thought of the warm hotel room with regret, and last night, after having a beer (it seemed to go right to my head) I went back to Barry's hotel room with him. He has a suite with a guest room. He might have been disappointed with me but I had not given him any illusions as to what I would do anyway. I am a virgin.

Istanbul, Turkey
Sunday, 14th March 1976

To travel like this has been my dream for so long. It feels so wonderful.

The bus has now stopped in Istanbul, in Turkey, and we are staying here four nights. I have come to know the people I am travelling with very well, and we have such good fun. There are about thirty people on the bus and I spend time walking about with different people every day.

We are staying in a little old hostel called 'Student Hostel' which costs seven and a half Turkish lira a night – about twenty-two pence in English money. An old Turkish man runs the hostel and lives in a cosy little room with a warm stove around which we sit in the evenings, chat, and drink tea which he makes for us, although he speaks no English.

I never thought Istanbul would be so cold and wet. I only have one woollen jumper with me and I wear it all the time. It must be filthy! A girl I met in the other hostel gave me an old cardigan which I also wear on top. It's a loose old thing. But somehow playing the pauper makes the game more fun! Everyone here dresses as though all their clothes come from a jumble sale, but it would be impossible to carry many, or 'good' clothes while travelling. Smart clothes would be ruined.

There is a cafe here called 'The Pudding Shop' which apparently is famous all over the world. All the young (freaky) foreign travellers collect there. The characters that spend time in this cafe are very interesting. I have done quite a bit of sightseeing here but many people sit in The Pudding Shop all day, where they actually can buy draught beer, quite something for Istanbul; however, I don't drink it. Yesterday I saw one boy in the cafe wearing one laced boot and one shoe – that is not a very strange sight in this place in comparison with other sights! My shoes are so dirty (it is muddy here) that the shoeshine boys that line the streets keep shouting over to me, and to the others. Their shoes are no better, but who cares about having shiny shoes here! At least none of my clothes are ripped like some people's are, and I do keep my skin very clean. I use deep cleansing milk. The air is so filthy here.

I feel free, as though I have at last spread my wings and am flying like a bird across the sky. I am restless to be flying further and further into the mysterious unknown, but somehow I feel protected.

Monday, 15th March 1976

How can I express the happiness I feel tonight both within and around me, a calm which fills my mind and soul? I am so thrilled that I have begun my journey to India. However, the cold rain and mud takes the pleasure out of sightseeing in Istanbul.

Yesterday I walked with Mike to the Bosphorus River through the zoo and park. One side of the river, our side, is Europe and the other side is Asia. I found the zoo shocking. Even cats and dogs are kept in cages. There are many birds, wolves and one camel. The animals look unkempt and the cages are too small, but then isn't any cage too small? In one cage there are about four bears – poor things.

In the afternoon we went to a museum and also the Sultan's Palace, a magnificent building, where we saw the Jewels of Turkey.

Here I am again, sitting in the cosy little room surrounded by my bus-mates and the dear old man who owns the hostel. I'll be quite sorry to leave here tomorrow morning.

This afternoon I went for a Turkish Bath! We have only cold showers in our hostel and so I asked the Turk who helps our group and changes money for us, to recommend a place. It cost fifteen Turkish lira (forty-five pence), but it was to me worth much more than that. I spent three hours of sheer heaven there. The saunas of Western Europe have nothing on the real Turkish Baths. It is such an old building, just like old Roman Baths. The bathroom is a round marble temple with a domed roof. There are marble pillars all around and large marble bowls with hot and cold taps on the walls with a kind of step to sit on. The air is warm and steamy but not too hot.

There were about five other women in there and I talked to an American girl who is also travelling alone. She ordered two teas for us. She has been teaching English in Tehran where it is possible to earn a lot of money apparently. Because the bath is not too hot like a sauna, it is possible to stay in the room for a much longer time, lying on the marble floor and ladling warm water with a bowl all over the body, throwing water everywhere. That appealed most to my childish mind!

When I came out I had photos taken for my visas (in clothes of course!) and then I went into The Pudding Shop and met my Turkish friend in there – a student doctor who took me around the bazaar when I first arrived. The bazaar in Istanbul is supposed to be the largest undercover bazaar in the world. It is quite fascinating, and everything has to be bargained for.

There are some wonderful carpets in the shops, also carved pipes and chess sets. There are many nut, sweet, and spice shops. I love the Turkish Delight sweets sold here.

Some of the Turks are very poor. I have seen a few beggars. I feel sorry for the shoe-shine boys sitting in the mud at the side of the roads. Also I saw a ragged little girl selling bird seed on the steps of a large building. Some parts of Istanbul are quite depressing, especially in this cold and rainy weather. It is a very freaky city around where we are living, perhaps also because we are here, or maybe I should say – so many young travellers like us are here! There is a second-hand clothes shop where people buy and sell.

Tehran, Iran
Monday, 22nd March 1976

My journey has changed completely now. I am now no longer on the Magic Bus! I need to recount my adventures from where I left off.

In Istanbul, an American got on the bus and sat next to me. His name is Paul. We talked quite a lot for he is also interested in writing and in reading. He suggested that we might travel together for a while.

Eventually we decided to get off the bus and make the trip alone taking local transport. We thought it would be more interesting as well as more of a challenge. We are now in Tehran waiting to take the bus tomorrow morning to Karbol, a small town on the way to Meshad which is near the Iran/Afghan border. We cannot get a bus directly all the way at this time because there happens to be a religious festival taking place – the Muslim New Year festival, and Meshad is a holy city, so many Iranians are going there and all the buses and trains are full. Seats have to be booked a few days in advance. As we don't want to wait so long, we are getting the first bus out to one of the towns along the way.

Tehran is not a very pleasant city. It's fairly modern, cleaner than Istanbul, but has little character. However, the women in their head dresses (like long cloaks) which cover them from head to foot, make it interesting. Very often they wear jeans beneath them. The material does not cover their face but as they walk along the street they hold it across their nose and mouth, especially if there are men around. Usually the cloth is made of cotton, is dark in colour but sometimes has small flowers printed on it.

When we were on the bus, we passed through desert lands, very barren with a few small villages in remote areas. The people there are very cut off from the rest of the world, and very poor – they live in mud dwellings. We saw few women – but many men and boys. We stopped for half an hour in one little village. The whole town turned out, surrounding the bus (no women at all). Men and boys of all ages stood around cheering and shouting as we got on and off the bus and as we walked about the village they observed us with curiosity. Probably our arrival was the biggest event in their day.

Some villages in Turkey appeared also to be very primitive, especially as we went further east. The women wear cotton pantaloons almost like pyjama pants with a tunic over the top of it, as well as the material wrapped around their heads and part of their faces.

When we arrived in Tehran and decided to get off the bus, we asked for some of our fare money back, and I was able to sell my rucksack straight away. (I had been hoping to do this because, with its metal frame, it is uncomfortable.) Here I managed to get twenty US dollars for it, and probably I could have got more if I'd bargained correctly. The family were quite wealthy and offered us a room free for a couple of nights, which was helpful as the youth hostel was full.

In the town I saw live chickens in metal rock-like cages in the street treated like lumps of meat as though they were dead. The cages were only big enough for their cramped bodies to lie in. Their heads stuck through the bars as the poor things stared out in fright and despair – it really showed in their eyes. They were carried by their legs unmercifully into the shops. I would not like to see how they are killed.

That evening we were taken by the family to visit their friends who owned a chicken farm; two buildings containing thousands of chicks feeding and squeaking, set in a huge garden with fruit trees. We were told that when the chicks are about sixty days old, they are sold, alive, to market stalls where they are killed. I didn't really want to go the farm at all, it made me sad. I didn't tell them I was vegetarian. I wished I had afterwards. The chicks were so sweet. I don't see why innocent creatures like these have to suffer through man's greed; it seems so unnecessary when there are so many vegetables, cereals, fruits, beans and nuts to eat in this world, instead of meat.

The next day we went on a bus to try to get visas but the Afghani Embassy was closed and yesterday we tried to hitch-hike out of the town. We made a pretty mess of the whole day really and spent far too much money on taxis going out to the road to hitch, and then to the bus station to enquire about buses. It seems difficult to hitch-hike here because many of the drivers demand money and ask for more than the bus fare. Also many Iranians were also asking for lifts because they have a holiday.

The weather has been fairly erratic, sunny sometimes, and very cold at other times. One of our friends on the bus caught a cold and lost his voice completely as I have now done! Losing my voice makes me feel vulnerable. I feel like shying away from people because I can't converse with them. I have spent more time reading the books I brought with me, *The Hobbit* and *The Agony and the Ecstasy* about the life of Michelangelo.

Wednesday, 24th March 1976

We are in Karbol, an Iranian town by the Caspian Sea, on the way to Meshad. We could not get a bus directly there from Tehran. Yesterday evening we were offered a lift from an Iranian (no, he was Turkish) but we are still waiting for him now. It seems that he has not shown up, so it looks as though we'll have to stay here another night. Karbol is a sweet little town, although I think it is not so little for an Iranian town. The bus ride here was quite eventful. My voice was twice as bad, or should I say – non-existent, so I had to sit like a stuffed cabbage all the time. I could only whisper, and Paul couldn't always hear me as there was so much chatter on the bus.

We passed through the mountains and some beautiful gorges. The scenery reminded me of Switzerland. There was deep snow, and pretty little chalets dotted the countryside. This area did not seem nearly so poor or primitive as that on the other side of Tehran. The snow was so deep and the roads so icy that the bus had to travel at a very slow speed, and stopped about three times during the journey for half an hour.

Each time a man had to get under the bus and fix something – then there was a flat tyre! No wonder the bus fares are cheap. The trip cost us 120 rials – less than £2.

All the women on the bus were covered from head to foot and everyone took great interest in us. It was a pity that I could not speak to them, but only make a gruff noise in my throat! At the end of the trip, piles of nut shells, paper and orange peel covered the floor. In these buses everything is thrown on the floor!

When we arrived here, we tried to find someone who could speak English. Of course, so many Iranians came up and chattered away in Parsi but we couldn't understand. Eventually, by chance, we found someone – a boy of eighteen. He had learned English by himself at home by means of a grammar book. Very funny English he spoke. It must have been (in fact it was, for we saw it later) an old fashioned, outdated book, full of polite phrases! He spoke very theatrically with much gesticulation and emphasis. The book even had mention of Queen Victoria, I noticed!

This boy was very nice to us. He came to speak with us while we were sitting in a tiny cafe. He worked in his uncle's photography shop next door. There are so many of these places – people must love photos! I don't carry a camera myself.

Someone must have told the boy that there were two English-speaking people next door. As always, we were the centre of attraction as we walked through the streets and wherever we went. The boy came into the cafe and introduced himself, bowing slightly and shaking hands. We asked him for some Iranian words as so few people speak English here.

Later we were invited to his house for dinner. We had to walk down a muddy lane to his house where we met his family – mother, father, sisters, brothers, nieces, nephews – all sitting on cushions on the floor around a low table. They were all very fat and the women wore long, unshapely dresses that draped unglamorously from their bodies and old, unattractive looking cardigans.

They led us into a second room, more luxurious looking, with a Persian carpet on the floor and a table laden with sweets and biscuits and oranges which they urged us to eat and eat. They brought tea also, but the dinner was taking so long to cook that after waiting for more than two hours we did not wait for the meal but left as we were both tired and feeling unwell. I felt guilty about leaving before the dinner was cooked but Paul insisted that he did not want to wait any longer.

We booked ourselves into a little hotel for 125 rials a night – each. We are still here. There are no showers, only taps, but it is quite reasonable and clean in comparison to other places we've stayed. However, if we have to stay here again tonight this is rather a waste of money and time, as we could have caught the bus this morning. Food and accommodation is comparatively expensive here. Last night at about 9.30 pm, the Turk, Ali, whom we had spoken to before, came in and offered us a lift. We managed to converse with him through our few words of Parsi that we have learned, sign language and picture drawing.

Paul and I had an argument last night – about sex of course! Since we came away from the bus we have shared a room but I realise this is probably a mistake. I like him but I am not in love with him. I don't want to have a physical relationship with him.

Thursday, 25th March 1976

We waited yesterday for Ali all day. The car was not ready. He paid for our hotel again last night and also bought us tickets for the cinema in the evening.

Just before we entered the cinema, we met the Iranian boy who had invited us to dinner. When we said we were going to the cinema, he immediately asked if he could come, telling us we were going to see the best Iranian film. Poor boy, he was mistaken about the film – he thought we were going to see a different one. I did too! It turned out to be a sex film as there were nude scenes in it, but it was very mild – I am sure it would never have been called a 'sex' film in Amsterdam. It was actually an old Italian film (about six years old) with Iranian sub-titles.

I was probably the only woman in the whole cinema. When the lights went on at the end, all the men turned and looked at me. After the film the Iranian boy went off home quickly. Probably he was disillusioned with us.

Ali has been very kind to us though I wish we had caught the bus. I hate all this waiting around. I want to get on with the journey!

Chapter Three
Adventures in Afghanistan

Herat

Saturday, 27th March 1976

Now I have a decision to make. Whether to go, or whether to stay! But there is a lot to explain.

We are in Afghanistan, Herat – and it is incredible! Like a different world – so different from Iran, so fascinating! Perhaps I should tell the story from the place where I left off.

Last time I wrote, Paul and I were sitting waiting for our Turkish friend. He took us to the shower in the morning and said the car would be ready by 11 o'clock. Twelve o'clock came and went, one, two, three o'clock. We were feeling so fed up that we left. I think his car was not yet ready – he was putting the engine in himself!

Then our bad luck finished for a while – for good I hope! We got a taxi to the bus stop and straight away, practically, a bus came along for Meshad. It was a tiny mini bus and held about twenty passengers. Some of them got out along the way, as did the one Iranian woman. The rest were men and they sang loud Iranian songs all night and offered us oranges. By morning we were exhausted, but after arriving in Meshad at 6.30 a.m. and catching a taxi to the right bus station, we got a bus leaving straight away for the border.

At the Iranian border there was a building at the back where we sat waiting while they checked our passports. Against one wall we could see a large glass case full of things discovered by the customs officers – containers of every kind that had been used by travellers for hiding hashish and other drugs as well as precious gems. The names of the smugglers were written on labels. They were probably doing long jail sentences in Iranian prisons – I pity them with all my heart. This case of smuggled articles probably served as a warning.

After the border, everything changed suddenly. There was a little mini bus to meet us with two Afghani drivers to take us the five miles from that border to the Afghani border. How different these people are, not only in their dress: scruffy turban-like head dresses and baggy pantaloons and tunics, but in their characteristics too. They are strong, wild, rugged people, but I feel respect for them – the men do not stare in the same unpleasant manner at me as the Iranians did as I walk along the streets. They are altogether nobler people, or at least so they appear, though perhaps I should not judge. They lead a hard, wild life here – they look almost like unkempt gypsies.

The Afghani border had one or two buildings set in the middle of desolate, desert-like country. The weather was freezing! That was yesterday. We had to fill in forms to show how much money we were taking in, and also show our vaccination certificates. One poor guy did not have a cholera vaccination certificate and was told he would have to stay there twenty-four hours after having a shot in quarantine. What a horrible place to stay. I went to the toilet there – it was a little mud building outside with a hole in the ground, but at least it didn't stink like those in Iran and Turkey.

After we were finished at the border, the same bus took us to Herat. The gravel road was narrow and the land we passed through was some of the most barren country I have ever seen, with only a few camels, goats and Nomadic tents scattered here and there. We saw groups of men riding camels laden with goods going along the same road. There was little traffic. On the bus there were a few Germans, English and Dutch as well as Paul and me. Our luggage was piled up on the roof.

The mini bus to Herat had a flat tyre when we were half-way there and we stopped at a little brick building in the middle of nowhere – most buildings are not of brick, but of mud. Tea was made for us – in glasses as usual – from a little teapot set on a stove that we all huddled around. We chatted to the Afghani men. They have a great sense of humour and answered my many questions. At least there seem to be quite a few people who speak English here. There were not in Iran.

We arrived in Herat late last night and all of us piled into the little hotel right next door to the bus station. The owner came out to meet the bus. The hotel is a simple wooden building with little furniture inside – bare wooden tables and benches in the restaurant – more like a hostel than a hotel. It costs 20 afghanis a night – about 20 pence. Paul and I got one room between us for this price. I am sitting in the little restaurant now. The food is very good. Last night I had rice, spinach and beans. The bread here is huge, oblong-shaped and flat – it is whole-wheat bread cooked in stone ovens on the ground with an open fire at the back.

I was longing to explore Herat last night but it was already night and too dark. I woke up this morning with the sun shining in – what a surprise – at least it wasn't raining or snowing. There had been deep snow near the border and for some way into Afghanistan. Paul got up very early this morning and went out but I didn't wake up until about 10 o'clock. I found out later that he had gone horse riding around the town. While I was lying in my sleeping bag – I slept on the same mattress as Paul but a little way away from him! – suddenly the owner of the hotel came into the room. He said he didn't know anyone was there! He said his name was Josef and he invited me to come for a free breakfast and talked to me about Yorkshire, where he says he stayed when he visited a woman tourist who once stayed in his hotel. Then he took me around the town.

What a surprise I got when we went out – what a beautiful little town! The buildings here are square with flat roofs and look as though they are made from sand. The town looks like a picture out of the Bible, from Biblical times, and the way of life here looks as though it has not changed since then. It is like stepping back two thousand years into the past. It is amazing here – so fascinating and picturesque. What a wonderful film setting it would make. It is like a place completely cut off from the rest of the world, both in time and space.

We caught a pony and trap, as one would a bus, to a little place where I changed some money. It was a restaurant, and Josef, the owner of my hotel, bought me some hot milk and tea. There was also a plate of sugared nuts. Then we caught another pony carriage to the bazaar – an incredible place with low arch-like stone or mud square buildings, open at the front, each displaying different goods. Inside, at the back, you can see the men and boys at work – some are carpentry shops, others are blacksmiths, others are bakeries, etc.

There are open 'shops' and stalls of nuts, raisins, dates and cakes of all kinds, although not like European cakes. There are Afghani dress shops full of long embroidered dresses of different colours, and fur shops.

This afternoon I went around the town with Paul. He bought a coat today for one hundred dollars – fox fur. He can probably sell it for three times that much in Europe or the USA. Everywhere we went, people pointed to our clothes and said, "How much?" They wanted to buy our western clothes. I sold my denim dress for 100 afghanis. Now I am wearing jeans and my black zipped jacket. We saw women's burkhas for sale (like long cotton cloaks) and one of the stall sellers asked Paul if he would like to buy one for me! We met a couple of western people walking around. The girl told us that her boyfriend had been made an offer for her. An Afghani man wanted to buy her – he had offered several hundred sheep for her!

Back at the hotel, Josef the owner, also asked me to marry him! Then he made me an offer. He said I could stay here free in his hotel for a few days – free food and accommodation – and that he would take me sight-seeing to the little villages around about, and out horse riding and bicycle riding – then I could catch the 'Overlander' bus that comes in five days' time all the way to India.

I thought I had better make things clear to Josef, as they apparently were not clear for Paul. I told Josef that I would not sleep with him. He promised me he did not expect that.

I would like to stay here a bit longer. I want to discuss it with Paul. I feel determined that I am not going to become dependent on anyone on this trip. Perhaps Paul would rather travel alone now he knows that our relationship would be virtually platonic. Certainly he has grown a little colder to me.

Sunday, 28th March 1976

I am still here in Herat. It is about 8 o'clock in the morning and I am sitting in the restaurant eating my breakfast – yoghurt, jam and flat whole-wheat bread. Paul left at 6.30 this morning. He took the bus for Kabul. I have decided to stay here longer.

From the window I can see the dusty, brown, dirt road and watch the people go by every now and again – sometimes a man or a group of men, sometimes a woman completely veiled. Not all the women here wear the kind of burkha that covers even the face, but many of them do. There is material with tiny holes or a mesh on the face part through which the woman can see out, but nobody can see her face. She is completely covered from head to foot in the roughly dyed garment. The colours vary – red, blue, purple, but are mostly dark.

There is no point in wondering whether I have made the right decision in staying here. I have done it now. I feel that I must play my life as an instrument – by ear, now! I must follow my instinct and hope that it will be a good guide to me!

Today I hope to go horse riding around the town like Paul did. That should be great fun. Whatever happens, I think I am glad I stayed and didn't leave with Paul. It would be so easy to develop an attachment to someone. I would always wonder just how frightened or insecure I would feel if I were alone. Now at least I will know!

Evening

Today was sunny but not terribly warm. However, I wrapped up well and I was not cold.

At 10.30 this morning I went out to get my horse. The owner of the hotel, Josef, took me there. He is a rough gypsy-looking man with a beard (like all the Afghanis) and wears pantaloon type trousers and a tunic as well as a turban-like scarf around his head. After walking down some dusty streets we entered the stables through an arch near the Afghani (not the 'tourist') market. How strangely primitive it is – mud walls and straw – all in the open air. We passed little open workshops where men were dyeing bundles of wool – rough sheep's wool in big pots – and we stepped over puddles. I asked for a quiet horse and was given a large brown one, rather too big for my liking. I am not used to riding and have only ridden a horse once in my life! I insisted on paying although Josef wanted to pay for me but I feel that I am taking enough from him, and anyway, I am not giving anything in return!

I hired the horse for one hour although I did not keep it that long. The horse was brought out for me and Josef helped me up onto it. From the one riding lesson I had had years ago I could not remember how to make the horse walk and stop. I believe the poor horse sensed I was nervous. It walked so very slowly that I thought it must be very old, and I bore with it, shaking the reins a bit sometimes to encourage it to go faster. Then suddenly I discovered it wasn't so very old after all – it started to charge off down the street at top speed. I was terrified out of my wits and screamed! All the people looked at me and some little boys were laughing. One had thrown a bucket of cold water at its back legs. I pulled the reins and the horse slowed down. Some more boys brought along another bucket of cold water and I shouted at them just as they were going to throw it, but when I wasn't looking, a boy with a donkey hit my horse on the back with a stick. Again it charged off down the street and I felt very saddle sore!!

I had ridden the horse all around the courtyard of the large mosque and market place. In the grounds, sheep and goats were grazing. When we came back around near to the horse's stables again, the horse started to run once more to get back into them and I held on for dear life! The stable owners led it out again for me, but after that, the horse was so nervous – it sensed I was – that after ten minutes I brought it back, greatly relieved to tread on solid ground again, though my legs were shaking like jelly.

Some shop owners then invited me into their shops to drink tea (of course with the intention that they might persuade me to buy some of their goods) and I accepted. In one shop I tried on a long, embroidered Afghani dress. There was a curtained off area in the corner. The owner of the shop peeped around the curtain just as I was undressing and he saw me in my bra! Afterwards he offered me a dress free (but I was afraid that there would be another form of payment expected afterwards!) One of the shop owners asked me if I had an Afghani friend – meaning Josef. Probably the news had got around the whole town that he was entertaining me in his hotel.

Today, later, when Josef came to find me and walk with me, he wanted to buy me a dress and was very offended when I refused it. I feel I am using him to take me around as it is. He tries to kiss me, but really I don't like him touching me. He is not so unattractive, but I am not attracted to him – he is so rough looking. Perhaps it is his habits. He spits on the ground a lot!

I think I should not always be trying to 'get what I can' out of people as I do when I am abroad and meet the locals! I thought it would be nice to be taken around Herat but really I would much rather go around by myself!

Tuesday, 30th March 1976

It is a real effort to keep up with all the news. There is so much life to live and now I feel I really am living in the present! Here life demands of me to be alert with all my senses awakened. Here, I must live totally, consciously, with absolute awareness – in this dangerous new world I am in. This is life at its rawest, most vital, most primitive. Everywhere around me people are living because they must. They are creatures of the earth, drawing their crude, simple survival from Mother Earth, struggling for what life might give them. Here I am thrown back to my original self. I can't act a part or a role – I have to be me as I really am.

Herat overwhelms me with this feeling. I walked around the town for three hours and the emotion it evoked in me was too much for me – it was overwhelming. I had to go back to my little hotel. I had to speak to some Europeans again – to do something familiar. Not only did I feel that I had stepped back two thousand years or more in time, but that I myself had changed, and I was frightened. I had the feeling that I might get stuck in a different space and time and might not be able to get back to the present, to my own conception of reality. This country is so different from anywhere I have ever seen on this Earth. People here are so cut off from the rest of the world it seems; as though they are living in a time warp.

I walked through the old Afghani markets and was the only European. I wore a scarf over my head. The women that walked the streets were all covered from head to foot except a very few old women who crouched down by a well or in a doorway here and there. There were just a few beggars. One old woman with only her eyes and top of her cheeks showing, crouched down with her hand stretched open. I gave her a ten afghani note (only about ten pence.) She closed up her hand slowly and stared up at me through the cloth wrapped loosely around her head, though I could not see her whole face. I think she was really poor. None of the Afghani passers-by gave her anything.

I saw the workers at the back of their little shops – though they can hardly be called 'shops', they are just open, narrow, square buildings, very small, each with a high arched front. There was primitive-looking jewellery in some cases and women's burkhas for sale. I went to look in an old mosque on a hill. On the hill opposite is an old ruined castle, very picturesque, and in the distance are mountains.

A soldier came up to me in the mosque courtyard. He spoke good English which he said he had taught himself. Within minutes he was asking me if I would like to marry him as he was a bachelor and would like an English wife! When I declined the offer he asked very politely whether I'd like to stay a night in his house.

Before I left the soldier, he talked to me about the people crouched down on the ground at the mosque entrance. There were three very old women. I actually got a glimpse of their faces though they drew cotton material across their heads which covered all but their eyes. Perhaps they were not so old. There was also a blind old man. The soldier told me that the women are very poor and that they clean the graves and ask for a little fee from the mourners – this is their living. They stared up at me as I stared at them. I felt we are like creatures from two different worlds – or should I say different universes – what could they know about the west?

For them it is another world that does not exist, one that they will never know.

I must have looked like an unreal character out of a book or a film to them – from the far-off west, in my western clothes: jeans and black-zipped anorak. As my feelings overcame me, I felt afraid. I wanted to go away quickly from this place. I gave the soldier a few afghanis to share among the women and blind man and he gave it to them and told them what I had said. He told me they would buy food for that evening with it. Everything is very cheap in Afghanistan but there is a tourist price and an Afghani price. A few afghanis (one afghani equals a penny) go a long way for them.

I felt a hypocrite giving them money. My life and theirs is so different. I feel that we can never 'reach' each other. How could I ever explain this feeling except by saying that in these moments I was overcome by fear?

As I hurried back to the hotel I reflected that life here is very cheap and that death here is as natural as life. It seems to me that human beings here are as creatures crawling on the Earth. They live and they die. They exist and they suffer, and they struggle with life. In the west we have it so easy in comparison – we don't realise it. I suppose it is as life was hundreds of years ago in Europe.

When I got back to the hotel in the evening, Josef, the owner, became a problem and would not leave my room. I became angry and said I wanted to pay my bill, food and all. Actually I remained very calm, but he didn't! He had promised me that there would be no strings attached, but he was not being honest.

Finally he took the payment. Afterwards he wanted to give me the money back and 'talk' about it, but I would not have it. I locked him out of the room and refused to answer, so he went away in a rage. I am glad I had not accepted that dress off of him; all he had bought me really was coffee and milk in shops and paid for me to travel in the horse carriages.

I bought a bus ticket for Kabul and set my alarm for five o'clock the next morning. The bus was going to leave at six o'clock.

After I had locked my door in my room for the night, I took myself in hand saying to myself sternly: "This is Afghanistan, not Spain – you had better act a little less stupidly!"

Certainly I blamed myself for what happened because I had been so naive in believing that the owner of the hotel was being so genuinely nice, and because I was really only using him for what I could get out of him – free lodgings – which I didn't get in the end! However, in the morning he said goodbye to me and was respectful again.

In one way, or perhaps more ways than one, it is a nuisance being a woman here. Mostly if men are nice to me, there is another motive, and yet the Afghanis are very naturally hospitable to strangers. They are helpful and generous to men travelling alone (as I've heard from other travellers) and to couples, though often they offer money for the girl, but they just can't believe that a woman can travel alone – though I am not the first woman who has ever done it, I am sure. They think it is strange, and also amusing.

When they ask if I am alone, I always say, "No, I am with friends," or "meeting friends in the next town." Always there are English-speaking westerners where I stay anyway – so I am not really alone. Because we are in the minority and all are about my age – my generation – we stick together a lot. I spend much time chatting to other travellers, especially in the evenings.

Kabul

Wednesday, March 31st 1976

I caught the bus to Kabul with some other Westerners – two couples – and all five of us got a taxi together to the Hotel Mustafa in Kabul where I am now staying. I have got to know quite a few others here – men. I could so easily find someone else to travel with but I don't want to now. I want to be free and meet new people everywhere I go – I meet far more people when I am alone. Today an Australian guy from the hotel took me out for a meal. It was really nice and I spent all afternoon with him walking around the bazaar.

There is another guy here in this hotel who was also with me in Herat. He wanted me to go to Benari with him on an excursion to a very old town in Afghanistan but I decided against it. For one thing it cost six pounds sterling in English money, and for another, I would have to stay in Kabul another day and night and I don't like it here very much. Kabul is more westernised than the rest of Afghanistan, and not very pretty. There are a few high modern brick buildings but most are very low, white shack-like buildings. The roads are concreted, unlike those in other Afghani towns, which are more like mud tracks, but it is so unlike a city. I think Delhi will be more modern.

The bus trip here yesterday took sixteen hours. It was so long, but interesting. On the way again we saw many nomadic tents, camels and goats, and sheep with their shepherds. The land was rugged and often desert, but in some places, though few and far between, it seemed quite well cultivated. There were some villages in the desert, though I would rather call them mud settlements than villages – they are so, so primitive. Houses are square and sand-coloured, with slightly rounded roofs and often joined together so that there is no distinction between one house and the next. Much of the desert country is very dry and barren. The road curved down to Kandahar and up again to Kabul. It was quite warm in Kandahar unlike the rest of Afghanistan though the days are getting quite sunny now.

Kandahar looked a beautiful and fascinating old town – like Herat. I nearly got off the bus there to stay for a night but decided against this, although I regretted the decision afterwards. Some of the other western people got off there. I saw no other tourists in the town. There were about eight of us on the bus. The rest were Afghani men in their Afghani costumes and turbans. They looked at me with fascination as I was alone, and asked me if I was with anyone (by means of sign language) so I pretended I didn't understand. Every time I touched my bag to get anything out, drank some tea from

my flask, or put cream on my face, they all watched me and it was quite amusing – I felt as though I was entertaining them.

About four times during the trip, and once at sunset, the bus stopped and three quarters of the passengers – all men –

got out to pray along the desert road. They laid down mats and bowed towards Mecca.

Until Kandahar, I had sat with an Italian boy who spoke some English. He told me such interesting things, both about travelling and about his life, and about gemstones, which I must relate later if I remember, but right now I must take a shower and go to bed as I have to get up and get the bus to Peshewar in Pakistan tomorrow morning early. We will be travelling through some wild country along the Khyber Pass. Today I bought myself a long, blue Afghani dress – navy blue silk with red and orange embroidery on the chest. It has long sleeves. I had to bargain for it in the bazaar, of course. I traded it for my denim skirt and I paid one hundred afghanis – one English pound – which I think was reasonable. I wanted a cool long dress to wear in Pakistan and India.

Chapter Four
Travelling through Pakistan

Saturday, 3rd April 1976

Here I am, sitting in the 'Retiring Room' of Rawalpindi station in Pakistan, in the middle of the night! I am wearing the long silk dress I bought in Afghanistan and I have my long wrap-around skirt draped over my head because the waiting room is full of staring men! I am the only woman here, and I am feeling unwell with a dreadful cold.

The men here are all staring at me writing, but nobody has bothered me. I am covered up from head to foot except for my face! I am waiting here to get the train to Lahore which leaves very early tomorrow morning. I can't rest because I want so much to catch up with my news and carry on with the story of my adventures so far!

I have seen a lot in Pakistan.

The Khyber Pass was a long, steep, winding road through rugged, dramatic, mountainous country. It stretches for about forty-eight kilometres from Afghanistan into Pakistan.

As soon as we went over the border, I felt as if I was in a different world from Afghanistan. The weather was hot, and the scenery much greener. The buildings at the border seemed much more westernised than those on the Afghani side. In the customs office, I was the only passenger on the bus to be given tea! The customs officers kept saying what beautiful eyes I have got (just because they are blue!) On the bus also were some Americans and Australians who had stayed in the hostel in Kabul with me. I went to a hotel in Peshewar with them. Green Hotel it was called, and cost five Pakistani rupees a night (25 pence in English money).

When I first entered Pakistan I didn't like it and decided I wanted to get through it as quickly as possible. The countryside here is green and beautiful in these northern parts but everything touched by man appears so dirty. It is primitive, so very primitive here in the country villages, and yet so was Afghanistan but I loved it there. Here, in rural Pakistan, the houses are like wooden shacks and the poor people look as though they never wash, nor ever wash their clothes. The houses and shops are mostly made of tree branches, mud and sometimes also stones. Some people even live in caves.

When I first crossed the border, as the weather was so warm, I wore my long wrap-around skirt (in the normal way) and a sleeveless, tight fitting T-shirt. Then, when I went to change money in the bank in the town of Peshewar, the bank clerk behind the counter grabbed at my breast. After doing that, he offered me a cup of tea which I refused! I also got jostled in the street by men. It was then that I realised that I had better cover myself up like the Pakistani women! I have heard stories from other western women who have had trouble from men here.

These people, especially in the countryside here, are so isolated, and so confined to their little villages and often so illiterate, that they know nothing about the west. It is only natural then, I feel, that when we are visiting their country, we need to try to understand them, to see through their eyes and to see them without prejudice. I love the Taoist philosophy that I read about in Amsterdam – to live in harmony with existence and with everything around us. This is what I want to do.

I think this is one of the secrets of life. When I wrote about my stay in Herat, I expressed that I was afraid and overwhelmed there. That was because I felt like an outsider. I wrote that I felt that I and the women there could never hope to 'reach' each other because we come from different universes. That is not true. I can 'reach' others if I step into their world for a while and become one with what is around me. This is empathy. Wherever I am, I want to live at peace with the people, in harmony with their world – and then my experiences will be much richer; then I will learn, as I am coming to learn very slowly, what it is like to feel with their hearts. I don't want to observe the life here as if I am just a spectator, an outsider watching a film. I want to understand more than that.

Every area of the world has its own conditioning. I think a Pakistani woman without her 'veil' would feel as a western woman would feel walking the streets bare from the waist upwards. Everybody gets used to the conditioning of their society. In Afghanistan though, the people did not seem to mind that I was not wearing a burkha like the women there – they accepted me as I was. However, my legs and arms were covered with my trousers and jacket, as the weather was much colder.

Men here in Pakistan appear to be more sexually obsessed than anywhere else I have visited. They are repressed and deprived of the company of women. I am sure that makes them worse. I believe that if men and women meet on an equal basis, then men will not see women as sexual objects, but respect them as human beings.

The food in the markets here does not look clean at all, but the local people eat it. Their bodies are obviously used to it.

They have grown up in this environment and they are probably more immune to the bacteria here than westerners are.

I have to be careful what I eat, but I have a trust that if I am positive and not afraid, then perhaps there is more chance that life will protect me and I will stay well and safe. That's what I feel anyway. For this reason I would never carry weapons with me. I have met western women that do. I met one woman travelling, who carried a box which, if opened, would explode and possibly kill someone. She showed it to me. It horrified me! I trust to life and I do not invite danger, nor expect it.

Now to get back to my story. I have diverted from it too much!

Green Hotel was very clean and I slept in the same large dormitory as the other travellers. There was a girl and her boyfriend waiting for friends to come. We went out to dinner together that evening. Afterwards I got talking to some other English people in the same dormitory – two guys. They actually live in Pakistan now, in a village called Madyan in the Swat Valley, and they raved on about how beautiful it is – urging me to go and see it. They had just come up to Peshewar for a holiday they said. They told me they had originally (a year ago) been on their way to India in a van, but had never arrived because they liked Pakistan, and especially this valley in the mountains, so much. I noticed also that local men were smoking marijuana there quite freely in that area and were buying it over the counter in pharmacist shops as a herb!

The Swat Valley in the Mountains

I decided that I would like to see this beautiful mountainous place, the Swat Valley of Pakistan, and discovered that an

Australian guy was going there the next day on the bus, so I asked if I could go with him. One of the English guys called Len gave me his address in the village. He told me that his girlfriend and her friend were there and would make me welcome in their little house if I would like to stay there.

Next day I set out with Ray. He was good company. I was glad to travel with him in the local bus and I thought I could never have travelled there alone, but the next day I came back alone and felt quite differently. I wore my long Afghani dress with my wrap-around skirt which is one piece of material over my head, as I am now, and I had no problems whatsoever. I felt perfectly safe, and no one stared at me at all. I met a Western woman wearing jeans and T-shirt on the bus who told me she had been raped in Pakistan, but she was still wearing jeans and a tight T-shirt! In my long, loose dress with long sleeves, and with my head covered, everyone treated me with great respect, and in the village where we stopped I was politely helped off the bus.

The journey there was terrifying! The bus driver bumped and raced at about seventy miles an hour along narrow mountain passes – overtaking everything in sight. I did not dare look out of the window. Every few seconds the air-horn blared out. I was quite frightened. Coming back I had a much more pleasant and slower ride.

The scenery was spectacular – mountainous and green with streams and waterfalls, wild flowers and blossom. When we stopped in the little villages on the way – we had to change buses twice – children rushed up to us trying to sell us bags of sliced sugar-cane. Everywhere we see that. It is quite good to eat and very juicy, but after you have chewed for a while, you have to spit out the wood. Up in the village of Madyan they sold delicious brown raw sugar balls that taste like fudge. I wondered what it could be at first. They keep it in sacks.

At last we arrived in the village. Ray went to stay in a very cheap 'hotel' – two rupees a night, and I went to find this little house where I had been invited to stay. It was a one-roomed stone dwelling, with a roof of thatched branches, mud and stone like all the others in the village.

There was a high stone wall around it and wooden gates. The women there observe strict purdah. I knocked on the door and when Sandy opened it, I showed her the note from Len and said that if it was not convenient I could easily stay in the little hotel. However, she invited me to stay there and I slept on the floor on sleeping bags that night and they chatted about the life in that tiny isolated Pakistani village.

When I first saw the English girls I got rather a shock. They wore very old, tatty, baggy clothes, looked very unkempt, and were squatting on the floor. They looked like hippies, but first impressions did not do them justice. Possibly they were just as put off by the sight of me, as my clothes (my bright blue long silk embroidered Afghani dress) were very clean and rather showy, as I realised afterwards, in comparison to people they see every day in the village, and have done for a year since they first came there.

One of the girls was my age, 22, and the other, Sandy, a few years older. They offered me some rice and then I went out for a walk along the valley with Ray. When I came back I chatted with the girls. Len's girlfriend, Sandy, who rented the house, had been a nurse for seven years in England.

Next morning I learned an incredible thing – the people in the village had discovered that she had medical knowledge (because one day she had dressed somebody's wounds) and they came to her every day with their ailments. She had a regular surgery and even supplied them with medicines and pills which she bought herself from the chemist.

She told me that the village people did not understand that dirt could cause infections and sometimes she had to give pills first, as well as emphasising that they must wash wounds. She had learned a little of the language and it was obvious that the people respected her very much. She dressed like the women and covered her hair when she went to the shops. There was a doctor, she told me, but the women were shy of visiting him and would not go, so they came to her instead. She would not see the men, only women and children. Some of the women brought her a few nuts or herbs in return for 'treatment'. She told me that for a long time she had tried to keep her nursing skills quiet but that it was impossible to keep anything quiet in that village.

The other girl, a friend, was staying there for a while. She had been very sick and was recovering from hepatitis and pneumonia together! The weather had been very cold but now was getting hot.

I wished that I had stayed longer in that village to learn more about the people, but as always I am restless to move on. Sandy showed me some of the beautiful embroidery done by the women in the village. In the morning one of the women living next door brought us a pot of tea and some round flat bread fried in a kind of butter – ghee, I think. Sandy told me she had brought it to us because I was there. She told me how very, very happy, friendly and giving the people were – so very poor – and yet always wanting to share the little that they have. Average wages she said, are about ten to thirteen rupees a week. (One rupee is less than five pence). She told me how she loved living in the valley like these poor people, eating the foods that are in season. She said to me, "Never have I had so little but never have I been so happy."

I said I will perhaps visit them again on my way back from India.

Tuesday, 6th April 1976

I managed to sleep a little on a wooden bench in the 'Retiring Room' in Rawalpindi, but I woke up next morning with half a voice once more and am still unwell now! Actually I had travelled by mini bus with Gus – an American guy I first met in the hostel in Kabul, who was also in the hostel in Peshewar while I went up north. Then we travelled together as far as Rawalpindi, where he had to pick up some mail, but he was sick and decided to stay in Rawalpindi to rest and look for a doctor. I was anxious to move on in spite of the fact that my cold was worse – in fact, especially because of that. I didn't want to be ill in Pakistan. I wanted to reach India before I was too ill to go at all, so I waited in that waiting room and in the morning I caught the train to Lahore alone.

It was an experience to ride on a Pakistani steam train in the women's carriage and see the women's faces! They took off their head dresses once they were inside. I had no seat and had to sit on my rucksack in the corridor. It got very crowded – women sitting on boxes and bags, and standing. There was a great family or community spirit among them. For the first time since I have been in Pakistan I met the wealthier people. They were clean, and wore fresh, clean clothes – the usual pantaloons and tunics. They draped their long head scarves over the back of their heads and shoulders while in the train. Nearly all the women had young children and babies in arms.

There were a couple of men in the carriage – fathers, but no more. It was obvious that men did not usually travel there. What a different atmosphere there was in that carriage from an English train carriage. The women chatted as though they had known each other for years and offered around nuts and sweets etc. which they were eating all the time.

There was a great feeling of 'oneness' amongst the women as they fondled each other's babies and patted each other's children on the head. A couple of times I had a baby thrust into my arms by a busy mother, or was expected to sit a child on my lap when the carriage was ridiculously overcrowded. There was no question as to whether one woman would look after another woman's child. We were all women together; all 'maternal' and all were, in their eyes, natural 'mothers'. It seemed to me that it reflected the attitude in this country that this is the only function of a woman – 'motherhood' – and that there is no other life than family life here.

As a traveller and a lone woman with no family or children around me, I felt strangely out of place – almost unnatural! I tried to act like a mother but somehow I felt that I was not one of them. I felt awkward, but I did my best with the children. Every now and then a couple of men selling drinks, sweets, and serving very sweet milky tea in a big kettle, would knock on the outer door of the moving train and demand entrance to the crowded carriage – which was ridiculous. The women grumbled but always let the men in, who stepped over everyone and everything with their wares. How they ever manage to climb along the outside walls of the train while it is moving I can't imagine – it must be terribly dangerous.

Some of the women spoke to me, smiled at me and offered me their nuts and sweets. Certainly I was treated as a guest of honour and with great interest. I was quite sad that my voice was so hoarse that I could barely talk to them. One young girl gave me a bracelet.

When we arrived at Lahore at about one o'clock in the afternoon, a passenger took me to the bus stop so that I could get a bus to the border. Crowds, literally, of people came and stood around me there as though they had never seen a foreigner before! They all stood around me in a circle asking questions: "Where do you come from?" "Where are you going?" etc., all smiling and pointing and staring as though in amazement and wonder. I don't understand why! Perhaps it was because my hair is very light brown or perhaps because I was a woman alone! Perhaps I looked radiant with excitement and happiness! I felt like a celebrity. Again I was sad that my voice was so hoarse and I could not really talk to them. Loads of people promised to help me, but all I wanted was to get to the border quickly and with as little fuss as possible for I was not feeling very well.

On the bus everyone was again staring at me and smiling for nearly the whole journey. They couldn't take their eyes off me and offered me sugar cane and nuts. They touched my hair and my head scarf. I was beginning to wonder if there was something wrong with me! An old woman sat next to me. (Again the bus was so crowded I was sitting on my rucksack in the aisle.) She was holding two roosters in her arms. Their heads were bent low as if they were sick but every now and again they lifted their heads and looked about with beady eyes – poor things. One young Pakistani girl chattered away in good English to me, practically begging me to go to her house.

Chapter Five
India at Last

Amritsar – Home of the Golden Temple
Wednesday, 7th April 1976

We arrived at the border at sunset, five minutes before the gate closed! I had to rush like mad and then walk about one hundred yards through to the Indian border. What relief I felt to at last make it into India without dying before I arrived!!

A wonderful feeling of euphoria swept over me once I was through the Pakistani border. The day was quite cool but not hot. It was beautiful weather, and there were greenery and wheat fields all around.

At the Indian border I was welcomed with chai (tea). Straight away I noticed the difference between the Indians and Pakistanis. The Indians here are Sikhs. They look noble and neat. They wear coloured turbans which are neatly and flatly tied, not like those untidy ones of the Afghanis.

Immediately I liked the Indian Sikhs. They look trustworthy and sincere. They treated me as a person and not as a sex symbol! Perhaps it is because they are not Muslims. They welcomed me to India but treated me respectfully.

I felt overjoyed to enter India and this feeling is still with me. This is a moment I have dreamed about for eleven years (half my life) and I have made my dream come true. Here I was, walking into India alone – yes, I wanted to cross that border alone – and India smelt sweet and fragrant with blossom. I was at last out of Pakistan. I felt as if I had been through a long tunnel and now was entering the land of my dreams on the other side. As I entered India I was overwhelmed by the feeling: "I have come home."

I like the atmosphere here – even though Amritsar is a very poor and dirty town. A new and different energy pervades the place, and I feel interested and excited, but as yet I have seen little of India. At last I have arrived and I have stopped on the first stage of my journey to rest in this lovely, new, modern youth hostel here until I am really better. I have been sleeping nearly all the time. There are not many people staying here.

From the bus station I took a rickshaw to the youth hostel. The rickshaws here are drawn by bicycle. They are tiny carriages – barely big enough to carry one person. I was afraid of falling out! What a lovely surprise I got when I arrived at the new hostel – it is very clean! I paid for a room to myself for 8 rupees (about 40p) as I was feeling unwell and I kept it for two nights.

Tonight I am feeling better so I have moved to the women's dormitory which is half the price. There is only one other person here anyway – a teacher who has been teaching English in Malaysia. She is making her way back to England overland. Yesterday morning I walked out to the bank to change some money. Here it is all right to wear my long wrap-around skirt around my waist with a sleeveless top – what a relief – and I went to find a chemist to get some aspirin to soothe my bad headache. My voice was still hoarse.

Amritsar is so crowded and I nearly got run over many times by rickshaws and bicycles along the narrow streets. It's not a very pretty town. There are some very poor, tumble-down stone houses – very, very low with slate roofs.

I entered what I thought was a chemist. It was in fact the surgery of a private doctor who gives free medical advice. I asked for some aspirin but he examined my chest – and gave me about four different kinds of pills to take. He gave me some water in a dirty looking red plastic mug and told me to take the first dose now, which I did.

Fifteen minutes later, after I had been to the bank, I had a black-out in the street and fainted! Suddenly all I could see was a misty white haze all around me and I could not stand up any more! I had just bought a notebook at a little stall at the side of the road when I came over dizzy and started to fall down. I managed to get a Sikh who was passing by, to flag down a bicycle rickshaw for me to take me back to the hostel. I couldn't even see it when it came!

There are very many rickshaws going up and down the narrow roads all the time. As soon as I was helped up onto the tiny seat I felt a bit better and when I got back to the hostel I slept all afternoon. I didn't take the other doses of pills then! But I took the other dose when I awoke this morning at six o'clock as I knew it wouldn't matter if I slept again then. I may save the third dose out of curiosity to find out what the Indian doctor has given me! The tablets haven't killed me anyway! They might actually have done me good. Certainly I have been feeling very unwell and tired and have had a fever. The tablets he gave me have at least given me a good sleep! I have enjoyed my rest here and am staying longer until I am properly recovered.

It's not too hot here in Amritsar and it is lovely and cool in this hostel with the fans. I have spent all day yesterday and today resting or sleeping. Today I also attempted to write some stories while I was lying here in bed! I have been drinking a lot – boiled water – I feel very thirsty much of the time. Tonight I had a nice vegetable dish in the hostel restaurant. The people working in the hostel are very nice to me.

Saturday, 10th April 1976

It is only a few days since I wrote in here but so much has happened. The longer I leave it the less I feel inclined to write because there is so much news to catch up with, but anyway let me recount my story from where I left off. In Amritsar I was ill, not just from a bad cold as I thought, but I really was sickening for something, although I am sure I got ill from drinking the tap water in that filthy glass that the doctor gave me in that surgery! I have had dysentery! It was horrible!

 I was feeling better and I spent the day, or half of it, with the school teacher also staying in the hostel. We went to the Sikh Golden Temple and lost each other there. It is a beautiful place surrounded by a moat. There were very many pilgrims there – some immersed themselves completely in the cold water, because it is holy water. Attached to the temple is a free hostel for pilgrims where I would have stayed if I had been feeling better. Also, the temple gives out free food at meal times and many poor people go there and sit on the ground in a courtyard and wait to be fed.

 I was invited to eat there and of course I could not resist the temptation to try the food, although I felt a bit guilty sitting cross-legged amongst all those poor people. We were given enormous, flat, gold-coloured aluminium plates. Food was brought around in dirty looking buckets: firstly rice – a stodgy, spiced mess was slopped down into our dishes, then a brown-coloured gruel with some kinds of beans in it. It was lukewarm and tasted horrible to me, like a kind of insipid gravy. That put me off Indian food for a while, but since then I have eaten delicious curries, so I realise that all the food in India is not like that! Also we were given chapattis which are round, flat, unleavened breads.

I forced the food down me, for I felt that it would be wicked to waste it in such a place. After we had finished eating they came around with the buckets again for second helpings. I pulled mine away quickly – they had already given me an extra large helping the first time, probably because I am a foreign visitor. Afterwards I went to the corner of the room to see where the food was cooked in enormous iron pots. The washing up was done with sand, not water – apparently that is more hygienic.

That night I had dysentery! It started with a fever. I was shivering and then I had stomach cramps. I was really worried – I thought I had appendicitis. I had dreadful diarrhoea and felt so horribly sick and faint that I could not see anything when I stood up – everything was like a white mist. I had a dreadful night.

My friend who was staying in the dormitory with me, made some ginger tea for me to help take my temperature down, which helped a little. In the morning I decided to call the doctor when I found I was passing blood. I was afraid I had something worse than dysentery. The people running the hostel were so nice. They called the doctor for me and he arrived late in the afternoon and gave me some tablets which gave me relief from the sheer hell I was suffering. I took them with boiled water this time! My temperature was still so high. I asked him if he thought I had become ill through eating the food in the temple, but he replied, "Definitely not! It must have been unclean water, or the food you ate in Pakistan."

For the next couple of days everything I ate gave me diarrhoea and my sight was affected so that I couldn't focus at all. It was really frightening – worse than the dysentery because I was so afraid that my sight was permanently damaged, perhaps because I had such a high fever. Slowly my sight has become normal again and how I appreciate it and thank God that I can see so clearly and enjoy the colours and beauties of the world, unlike the poor blind beggars I saw on the train. I thought that my sight was only partially gone but even that thought was too terrible for me to bear.

It has taken me three days to feel better and now I have bought my train ticket for Delhi.

Agra – Home of the Taj Mahal
Sunday, 11th April 1976

I have had a very hot, nine-hour journey. Travelling on a train second class is very uncomfortable with hard wooden seats – but it is very cheap. The people on the train have again been very friendly to me. I got out my sleeping bag for an old woman to sit on – those long journeys must be terrible for old people. By the end of the journey there were several people sitting on boxes on the floor in our tiny compartment. I had a seat because I had reserved one – it's the only way to get a seat here. You have to pay extra, about one rupee (6p) for a reservation.

I noticed the difference in dress between Indian and Pakistani women. Indian women wear beautiful saris instead of pantaloons and tunics. There were some enormously fat women in the carriage with huge stomachs rolling out of their saris (bare midriffs). One very fat family sat in the carriage with several tins of homemade cakes (like large lumps of very sweet fudge) which they kept handling. They were obviously taking them as a gift to someone somewhere. They opened the tin and gave me some to eat – very over-sweet they were. No wonder the whole family was so fat. The tea here is over-sweet too. They boil the milk with the tea and spices and put loads of sugar into the teapot before serving.

The trains and station platforms also are like a circus, with people calling out their wares and selling cooked and uncooked foods, and cups of tea (called chai) in rough clay pots at every station. I looked through the window and I saw that people were actually sitting on the roof of the train and hanging on for dear life. I even saw people walking on the roofs of moving trains. I think it is not really allowed but the station staff turn a blind eye to it. I wonder how many people get killed that way. There were people crossing the railway tracks by foot and jumping off trains while they were moving, hanging onto the doors.

I met an English guy on the train dressed in orange clothes wearing a wooden necklace of beads around his neck with somebody's photograph on it. I asked him about it and he told me that he belongs to an ashram in Pune and this is the picture of the spiritual Master who lives there. His name is Osho★. It happens to be the same Master whose book of discourses I saw in Amsterdam – *My Way, The Way of the White Clouds*. I told him I would like to visit the ashram when I am on my way back up the west coast of India on my way home. He told me I should wait until the winter as it is too hot to go there now in the hot season, but I told him I will not be in India in the winter. However, he said there are people there now who stay all year round.

It is obvious that I have chosen the wrong time of year to come to India – in this, the hottest season. However, I am not going to worry about the heat, I am just going to travel around wherever I want to!

On arrival in Delhi, I took a little three-wheeled open taxi (a motorised rickshaw) to the youth hostel and found it closed, so the driver has brought me to a cheap hotel he knows in old Delhi. He grossly overcharged me for the ride even after I argued and complained and bargained. Now I make certain I never get into a rickshaw before the meter is switched on so they cannot cheat me. I have also got wise to prices, I know how much to pay rickshaw drivers. They always try to charge foreigners more – they think we are wealthy and ignorant of prices. I always find out average prices before paying out any money.

Monday, 12th April 1976

The little hotel I stayed in last night has suddenly been closed by the police. We were all turned out early this morning. I heard that they are closing a lot of the cheaper hotels, perhaps because some of the travellers staying there smoke hashish. Anyway, I had so many bites when I woke up – probably bedbug bites – that it is probably a good thing we had to move. I have moved with a couple of Australian guys to another cheap hotel recommended by a rickshaw driver. It is cleaner here and I have my own room for eight rupees a night. There are about twenty rupees to the English pound at the moment. When we arrived we immediately went out to eat in a little cafe and were met by the owner of a music shop nearby. He invited us to see his sitars made by his own craftsmen on the premises and then invited me to be his guest for lunch.

Thursday, 15th April 1976

For the last two days the owner of the music shop has been taking me sightseeing around Delhi paying for my meals and taxis. The good food has done me good. I feel completely healthy and fit again now but my host got to be a bit of a nuisance at the end and I am afraid I left this evening without saying goodbye to him. He was trying of course to arrange for us to stay somewhere together and wanted to take me by car all over India which I do not want. He was also getting terribly domineering and possessive. I don't want anybody dictating to me or ruling it over me! I need my freedom and I want to be my own boss.

Friday, 16th April 1976

I have taken the evening train to Agra. It is a much more pleasant journey than my last train journey – much cooler, and will only take a few hours. I spent most of the day before leaving Delhi walking around a shopping bazaar. I bought myself another long skirt for twenty-six rupees. I wanted another cool top to wear with it and I saw a little black sari top in a shop. I tried it on but it was too big for me. At once the shop keeper offered to alter it to fit me for twelve rupees, so after he had measured me I went away for an hour while he altered it on his sewing machine. I found a cheap, clean restaurant and had a delicious enormous salad for two rupees (ten pence).

When I went back later to have an ice cream and drink, the manager (or owner) called me into his office, chatted to me for half an hour, ordered me a meal and a huge ice cream sundae and also cancelled my own original bill! He also invited me to stay in his place. Unfortunately – or luckily! – I was able to say truthfully that I was leaving Delhi on this evening's train, but he gave me his card and told me to come and stay with him when I return to Delhi later.

If I was willing to sleep with anybody, I could stay in India indefinitely without any money at all, travelling around, but unfortunately I don't want to live like this! I have met some girls that do. I would hate to have to tag around with someone all the time just because I am indebted to them.

Monday, 19th April 1976

I am now staying in Agra, home of the Taj Mahal. I have met a very nice young Indian man here. I have enjoyed a couple of moonlit nights with him sitting by the Taj Mahal. Seeing it by moonlight is wonderful. It is entirely built of white marble and is regarded as one of the eight wonders of the world. It is a mausoleum created to house the grave of the Mughal Emperor's wife and was completed in 1648 C.E. It took twenty-two years to build and cost thirty-two million rupees, I am told.

The Indian friend who accompanies me here in the evening is very sweet and gentle and treats me with respect calling me Madam! I don't mind him kissing me – he does it so nicely. He works in the Travel Agency at the Clarks Shiraz Hotel where I go to swim in the pool. It's wonderful to swim in the cool water in this hot climate. He has a university degree and a Bachelor of Education degree too but he works in the hotel because he earns more there than he would elsewhere and he has to look after his old mother. He tells me he earns six hundred rupees a month and teachers in India earn half that – that is not more than eighteen pounds a month!

When I was travelling here on the train, I asked the people in my compartment (all men for a change) if they knew of the guest houses in Agra mentioned in my book, *India on $5 to $10 a Day*. One man suggested that I stay in a cheap little place owned by a friend of his in the same road. When we arrived in Agra he kindly ordered a rickshaw and took me to the place, which wasn't too bad as cheap Indian guest houses go.

I was invited into the man's house for a cup of tea before we reached the hotel and I met his wife and children. They live in one small room with two beds – one for him and his wife, and another large bed for the three children – a small girl and two little boys. There was a mosquito net right around their bed. Their mother gave me tea and homemade sweets, and then I went to the little guest house where I was the only tourist and was made quite a fuss of. I was glad when they gave me a padlock for the door when I asked for one.

The first night they asked me for twelve rupees for a double room (after I complained that fifteen rupees was too much.) The second day they gave me a single room for eight rupees after some Indians had left. I noticed in the book that some people paid ten rupees in that hotel – it's necessary to make a fuss about the price or they charge as much as they like and put the price up for tourists who look wealthy! I think I don't look rich, but anyway, they think all foreign travellers have money.

I wanted to visit one of the schools in Agra – there seem to be plenty – because I wanted to find out about teaching here. I asked a rickshaw driver to take me around, and stopped him at a little Methodist mission school where I asked if I might speak to the principal. I was shown into the pastor's house and invited to sit down and chat. His wife is the headmistress. I showed her my School Teaching Certificate and she said she would be pleased to have me as a teacher in the school, and if I could obtain permission to work in India, they would pay me. She said that the new school year starts in July after two month's summer vacation.

The family invited me to meals on Easter Sunday and suggested that I stay for a couple of nights in their attached Methodist mission guest house. Here I met the Reverend Powell – an American missionary who lives here. I am pleased be able to stay here as it is very cheap and clean – quite a luxury in comparison to the other guest houses I have stayed in in the heart of the village.

Tuesday, 20th April 1976

I have really enjoyed my stay in Agra, riding around on the little bicycle rickshaws. One day I went across the river to visit Baby Taj – a beautiful monument built to the same design as the Taj Mahal but smaller and more delicate. The river is fascinating. I saw many buffaloes bathing in the water. The sunsets over the river here are beautiful. The day I spent with the pastor and his wife was very pleasant and the Indian curries she cooked for lunch and dinner were fantastic. I felt quite guilty telling her I was vegetarian when she invited me. She cooked vegetarian meals for me – egg and fish curry (though fish is not really vegetarian). The food was so tasty. She dressed me in a sari too in the evening.

This morning I visited the school which was a very interesting experience. It started at 7.30 in the morning. I dragged myself out of bed at 7 o'clock. The temperature was pleasantly cool at that hour. The bell rang and the children lined up – all in their little school uniforms, maroon and yellow. The boys even wear maroon trousers. Children here seem smaller for their age than English children. Before school started the children said prayers for a few minutes in the playground.

Lessons went on until 10 o'clock when there was a short break. After that the nursery (kindergarten) classes went home. The other children stayed until 12.30 pm, when school finished. The morning was broken up into 35 minute periods and lessons were very formal. I suppose they have to be – some of the classes have nearly seventy children in them! The nursery class (three to five year olds) has sixty-eight children in it. The children were having end of year exams – even the nursery class! They were mostly recitation tests. The school is English medium. I stayed and observed all the classes. In one of them, all the sixty children were sitting doing nothing while each child went up to the teacher individually and recited a rhyme in English – this was part of the exam! The teacher was giving them marks out of 30.

However bad I think the very formal rote method of teaching is, and it is, I have to admit that it seems that the children learn very quickly to speak and write English. Even children in the nursery class were reciting little rhymes and could answer simple questions and obey commands in English even though it is not their native tongue. In the first class (children aged five to six years, though some older children are kept down) the children counted to a hundred and then wrote the numbers. The same test was on practically every page of their number book. It looks as though they do this every day!

I spent some time talking to the teachers – mainly a young staff wearing attractive saris. They were very friendly to me. Afterwards I visited the school craft department. Here the children speak only a few words of English. Their lessons are conducted in their mother tongue. The craft department is incredible. They make beautiful carpets and bags. When the boys leave school, if they can do nothing else, at least they will know a craft and perhaps be able to set up their own little workshop.

This afternoon the jeweller in the hotel shop here got me free entrance to the hotel swimming pool and invited me to lunch tomorrow. I have also been invited to dinner tonight by another jeweller who exchanged my watch for two black star ruby rings. I have been informed by other travellers that apparently it is possible to sell these gems in Europe for three times the price paid here. Well, it's worth a try, and I paid nothing for them.

Just now I was invited to watch the Indian dances at this hotel free of charge – it usually costs 20 rupees! One of the men who works in the hotel just came up to me as I was sitting here writing this diary, and told me I could go free to see the dances. I don't know whether I will get to the dinner in time though! All the Indians who work in this hotel know me as I've been swimming in the pool four times now.

Wednesday, 21st April 1976

Last night I went to the jeweller's shop as I had been invited for dinner and I had a horrible experience. I should have known that there was something strange about the owner inviting me to his shop in the evening after it was closed.

When I got inside, he locked the door and started trying to fondle me and made suggestive, crude comments. It was obvious what he wanted but I was having none of it. He offered me an emerald ring but I refused it. I was a bit scared but I remained calm and finally firmly reminded him that he had invited me for dinner and I wanted to eat. I was playing for time! He called through the bars of the window to a boy passing by, asking him to fetch a take-away meal from the restaurant down the road! I then managed to get hold of his keys which I saw in his pocket.

I purposely acted as if nothing was amiss and kept them in my bag saying I was waiting for the food. When it came I ate it even though it was a shabby kind of meal. I did not want him to see I was afraid. I had the feeling that if I panicked then he might become aggressive, so I remained centred and calm. Amazingly, after I had eaten, he let me open the door with the key and allowed me to go out. I think I was lucky because I could have been raped there. I might have been in grave danger. I remember that girl I met in Pakistan who said she had been raped.

Chapter Six
Varanasi – a Holy City

Friday, 23rd April 1976

Here I am in Varanasi in the midst of all the Hindu temples I wanted to see, but am spending the day and probably tomorrow too, stuck in a hot hotel room again like I was in Amritsar – typical! Something else had to happen! Now at least I don't have dysentery, or worse, but I have sprained my ankle after falling down a hole last night in the uneven old streets, and it has swollen up double the size. I can't walk on it at all. At the moment one of the boys who work in the hotel is massaging my foot with ice. I asked for ice and a bucket of water which is good for sprains and swellings – probably it won't do much good now anyway. I hope he won't ask for ten rupees afterwards – I didn't ask him to massage my foot.

I was so angry last night. After I had sprained my ankle and we took a rickshaw back to the hotel (I am sharing a room with a German guy called Genaut whom I met on the train from Agra) the rickshaw driver took us a long way round in order to get a bigger fare. (Admittedly he didn't know I had hurt my foot. I should have told him.) He asked for six rupees which we didn't pay. One of the drivers did that to me in Agra when I wanted to visit the Taj Mahal bazaar. It was an interesting ride through a little village, but I was angry that he tried to cheat me. I had been there several times before and knew the way. I paid him the normal price and actually an extra fifty paisa, and flatly refused to pay any more. Some of the rickshaw drivers are quite honest and then if the price is cheap I sometimes tip them if I am feeling generous. Some Indians are very helpful – sometimes too much so, and many are a pain in the neck!

I was feeling so fed up this morning about my sprained foot because there was a power cut for three hours from about 4.30 in the morning and the fan stopped working. It was unbearably hot and I sat outside the room on a chair as that was a little cooler and spent my time watching the dawn and brushing away the thousands of mosquitoes. The pain in my foot was bad enough but the heat was worse! I decided then to fly home as soon as possible – just as I did when I had dysentery – but afterwards of course I reconsidered and decided that if I fly anywhere it will be to the Himalayas, to a cool climate where there are beautiful surroundings and I can rest my foot for a while!

After that boring information about my left foot I shall recount the story from where I left off – and I do have a lot to express, in way of events and also feelings.

I had dreaded the train journey from Agra to Varanasi, but in fact it was pleasant. I had reserved a sleeper on the night train leaving at 9.45 in the evening, and it arrived here at about 2 o'clock in the afternoon.

The compartment was not overcrowded for a change and there were two bunks free – also fans which went off at night with the electric light! But at least a cool breeze came through the window. I saw Genaut on the platform looking for his reserved place. Our names were written in Hindi on a list on the side of the train. I had already found my place with the help of another Indian passenger. I was pleased to see another European travelling on my train and we discovered that we had bunks in the same compartment.

The bunks were like wooden benches – very hard – so I was glad I had my sleeping bag to lie on. At night I always put my handbag (the very large green zipped cloth bag I made out of some of my mother's curtain material) with my passport and my money, at the bottom of the sleeping bag at my feet to keep my valuables safe. I never leave my handbag alone anywhere during the day either – I carry it everywhere. It has all my money in it!

In our compartment there was also an Indian family – a young girl in a sari with her husband and young baby. There was a corridor in the train and no door which closed on our compartment. Along this corridor came beggars and boys carrying nuts, drinks, ice creams and meals for sale at every station where the train stopped. There were a couple of blind beggars and a man with hands amputated. I have seen some terrible sights here in India – and some conditions that could be treated in the West. I have seen many people sleeping on the platforms. Perhaps they are waiting for trains or perhaps they are homeless.

The stations are always so crowded, and as I said before, they remind me so much of fairgrounds. Most of the trains are old steam trains and are very noisy and smoky.

On the journey the train passed through some villages – primitive places with huts. I saw a well in one village like those I saw in Afghanistan. The countryside was quite dried up and sandy, perhaps because it is the hot season, but apparently this is one of the hottest plains in India.

When we arrived in Varanasi we took a rickshaw to a cheap little hotel mentioned in my book, *India on $5 to $10 a Day*, but it was full so we came to this place recommended by a rickshaw driver where Genaut and I are sharing a room – it's cheaper to share – fifteen rupees between us. We have our own

Varanasi – a Holy City

toilet (Indian style – a hole in the ground which is tiled) and shower, but of course it is not luxurious.

I feel a bit uneasy about sharing a room with a man again. Sometimes I wish there was no such thing as sex then I wouldn't have to worry about refusing – whether it is expected of me or not! However, Genaut is nice and is not demanding anything from me. He was doing research work in chemistry at a university in Japan where he spent two years. He is on his way home to Germany, spending some time in India. He can now speak Japanese!

Yesterday afternoon, after we had showered after the hot, sticky journey, we had a meal in the little restaurant and had to wait ages for it. They certainly take their time. I had cheese and peas curry with rice – large lumps of white stringy cheese which has not got much flavour – it is called paneer. One thing that is very nice here in India is lassi, a drink made with yoghurt and shaken up with a little milk and sugar and sometimes lemon.

After we had eaten, we went out walking – what a town! Actually it's a city, but like all Indian cities that I've seen, except Delhi, it appears more like a large village. There are so many bicycles and rickshaws that it's a real problem to cross the road or even walk along the narrow streets. Indian towns are the picture of chaos in no small way. There are market stalls everywhere, and flower stalls selling offerings for the temples. There were more of these as we got nearer to the River Ganges.

There is food being cooked and sold at the sides of the roads, cows and bullocks walking the streets, dogs lying around everywhere (some very thin), monkeys in the trees, and temples of all shapes and sizes – some are low and triangular and some consist of many tiny towers like asparagus tips ascending from the roof. The buildings along the roads here are often very elaborate, very crowded together and shabby with numerous balconies and pillars – queer looking.

Hundreds of people crowded the streets where we were walking. Then suddenly we came upon the river. There are steps leading down to it. It is the sort of sight that I had to stop and gaze at: it was evening and the water seemed to be shrouded by a misty haze. There were people everywhere crowding the steps, diving into the filthy water – Mother Ganges  – holy river! There are dirty straw parasols under which holy men sit by the water, and hundreds of people sit listening and talking with them. There are small Hindu shrines with idols inside at the water's edge, and lots of wooden boats filled with people going up and down the river. Never have I seen a sight like it – it took my breath away.

Again I had the sensation of fear and wonder that I had felt in Herat, Afghanistan. As Genaut said, we feel this way because we are experiencing something we have never known before. Suddenly it is thrust upon us as though we have been whirled away to another planet, to another universe, and we are trying to identify with it, to understand this other world, but there is nothing in our minds with which we can associate it, so we cannot relate with it, and it frightens us. I am glad I am not alone here.

Varanasi - a Holy City

Many of the boys and old men are dressed in shabby loin cloths – a long piece of dirty-looking material draped around their waists – particularly by the river. Women wear shabby-looking saris. We walked along the water's edge on the uneven steps crowded with stone shrines, idols and high and low temples. Then we came across the funeral burning spot – the Ghats. About five or six bodies were lying on the 'beach' steps, shrouded and tied like mummies. Some were already placed in piles of wood ready to be burnt, and there were three fires already burning.

Sitting on the roof tops are large vultures, waiting – for bits of burning flesh to eat, I suppose. I have never seen vultures before. I also saw rats scuttling about. People sit around everywhere – everyone looks poor and shabby and there are many old people. This is a holy city where people come to die. Many old and sick and crippled people stay in the free pilgrim houses until they die and their bodies are burnt; their ashes are then thrown into the water.

It is said that if you die in Varanasi you will go straight to Heaven. Dead children are apparently just thrown in the water without being burnt – their bodies just float down the river. I saw quite a few shrouded bodies being carried towards the water's edge.

During the whole time we were walking, an Indian boy accompanied us, giving a running commentary. Afterwards he asked us to come and see his handicrafts – of course, that was the reason for giving us the commentary! He invited us into his house for tea and we climbed a lot of steps above the water's edge to his little house in one of the tiny, dirty streets. In the house we saw an incredible loom where silk saris and shawls are hand-made – wonderful designs in gold thread.

The house was poor-looking but I don't think the family were so very poor. The boy told us that they sold their shawls to the Government, and many were exported, and he said they had many looms in different houses. He said we couldn't buy them from there, and that their designs were secret, but this was his clever way of trying to make us interested in buying the shawls, for he then said that maybe he could possibly allow us a couple of shawls at a cheaper price. However, we couldn't afford to buy anything.

When we came out of his house it was dark. That was when I slipped down an uneven step into a hole and wrenched my ankle. It was so painful and still is, although I've rested it all day. Never mind! At least no bones are broken – it could be worse. I appreciate every part of my body and all my senses now I am in India because of the dreadful sights I've seen. I realise more than ever that the most precious thing anyone can own on Earth is health of body and mind.

Saturday, 24th April 1976

Varanasi (or Banares as it is also called) is fascinating, yet somehow horrific at the same time. There are so very many poor people, bad conditions, and the streets are so dirty. I both hate Varanasi and like it because it is so interesting, so incredible, so strange and also so frightening for me. I feel that I am very close to death here. Life seems very cheap: human life – two a penny, and I feel sickened and depressed. Perhaps most of all it is the attitude of resignation and apparent lethargy of the people.

I rested my swollen foot for the whole day yesterday, but today Genaut and I took a guided bus and boat tour around the town as I couldn't walk. The bus left at 5.30 in the morning, the best time in the day as it is cooler. First of all, the bus took us to the market place – as near as it could get to the water's edge. The streets are so congested and we had to walk (I limped!) to the Ghats to board the little boat which took us up and down the river. Our guide answered our questions which were many.

At that early hour the river-side was buzzing with life as the sun was rising. Loud Indian music blared, and people crowded the Ghats (steps), bathing and talking to the priests and holy men. Some were doing yoga exercises and a thousand other things. Many were chanting or praying and other ascetics were practising austerities. I saw a man lying on a bed of nails and another man standing on one leg in the water. His leg was so swollen that it was huge, and we heard that he has been standing like this for years. He is worshipped by the masses as a saint just for this. What kind of religiousness is this?! It is so life-negative – there is nothing beautiful in it.

The boat took us further up the river where we saw women washing their clothes and a yogi who sat meditating. In another place some Muslims bathed. To them the river is not holy. Our guide told us that the water has been analysed. It is filthy, but freshwater fish swim in it and the locals drink it safely because it has a large percentage of sulphur in it which keeps it very clean.

When we got out of the boat, a holy man took my hand by the river-side and proceeded to read my palm. He said to me, "Soon you are going to find a treasure – soon in a few weeks, in July." I had not wanted my palm read, but I placed a few coins in his hand reluctantly. What kind of treasure can I find in India?! It can only be a treasure of the spiritual kind surely!

After the boat trip we were led through the maze of little cobbled streets – so narrow, only about five feet wide – to visit a couple of temples. There are hundreds of small temples as well as large ones – all different shapes – and shrines, flower sellers and sweet sellers selling offerings for the temple gods. I would not touch those sweets – they are balls of sugar swarming with flies. Much of the food being cooked in the streets is covered in flies. There are so many little stalls cooking rice or selling curd or fried cakes in dirty containers. There were pathetic-looking people lying around. The temples and shrines are the homes of idols – in some of them the god sits in the middle of the pyramid-shaped construction and there is barely enough room for the devotees to crouch inside and lay flowers and sweets. Some of the people here appear to be living in cubby-hole type buildings also – perhaps they are pilgrims. I hope they do not live in those holes permanently.

I have never seen anybody actually starving, or any very thin people, but there are some people with stunted growth and deformed limbs, and probably many suffer from malnutrition. I saw a starving dog which was a horrible sight – the poor thing was desperately searching for food. I bought it something and threw it down for the dog, but probably that merely prolonged its suffering. Some animals including dogs, look quite well-fed and I am told some people feed stray animals as a religious duty. In Varanasi there are many dogs lying around in the heat looking lethargic, apparently sleeping, like the people who often sleep in the streets.

We climbed back into the bus which took us to a little restaurant to have breakfast, and then the bus took us to four more temples slightly outside the town. The first, dedicated to Mother India, is an interesting temple with a large three-dimensional map of India carved in marble on the floor; and then we were taken to two modern Hindu temples. They are majestic places and remind me of pictures of ancient Greek temples I have seen with their idols at the front altar. Hindu scriptures are written on the walls and in one there is a mechanical holy man with moving lips and hands in a glass case reading from the scriptures – it is all very strange. I was told that previously a holy man used to sit and read from the book, but now there is a waxwork.

Upstairs in one temple there was an exhibition – it reminded me of a children's fairground show, or something out of a ghost train ride at a fair, for in glass cases were all kinds of mechanical models of demons, evil spirits and gods, moving backwards and forwards with flashing lights – telling stories from the Hindu scriptures.

Afterwards the bus took us to the new modern University of Varanasi. Genaut stayed there to look at it and I went back with the bus to rest in the hotel. My foot was hurting.

Sunday, 25th April 1976

It is so hot! Why oh why didn't I come to India earlier? There is so much I wanted to see but I can't bear to walk around in this terrible heat, especially with this sprained ankle! I am going to the hills where it is cooler. I have booked a seat on the train. Genaut is going to Calcutta first. He suggested that we travel together but I want to go to the mountains now. We have agreed that we will meet when he comes to Darjeeling in a few days.

Tuesday, 27th April 1976

Sometimes I wonder why I've come so far to see the dirt and poverty. It seems to me that here Mother Earth never closes her eyes, she embraces all: the good, the bad, the great, the low, the beautiful and the ugly.

I have dreamed of coming to India for half my life. I always thought I would find something here. I thought it was my destiny to come to India, but what really is there to find here? I have seen such terrible sights in India already and I have only just begun my travels around the subcontinent.

The wheel of life goes on turning and turning. This place is beyond time.

Chapter Seven

The Majestic Himalayas and Tibetans

Sunday, 2nd May 1976

Now I have found something beautiful in India! I have just spent five days in the mountains, in what must be one of the most beautiful places on Earth, scenery-wise. It is Darjeeling, in the Himalayas, on the edge of Nepal, north-east corner of India. It is so cool here that I had to get out my jeans and jacket – what a change not to be sweating every minute, all day and all night. But I'm going back to it today – I wonder why?! – I am dreading my next stop, Calcutta, but I must see it. I am now on the train, but I will recount the story from where I left off.

I was going to meet Genaut in Darjeeling, but he has not arrived yet and I have now left. Perhaps I should have waited longer, or perhaps he heard about the rainy weather in the mountains and decided not to come.

How can I ever come to terms with my crazy feelings? When I was with Genaut I wanted to get away because I was afraid of the relationship I thought he might be expecting from me. I thought that like Paul, with whom I travelled in Iran, he would be shocked to find out I am a virgin, and would therefore soon tire of me. We wore no clothes in the hotel room because it was so stiflingly hot. But Genaut was different from Paul – I realise that now and he had not had an American upbringing. He was very sweet. I ran away from him and there was no need. He just seemed to like my company. I think he understood how I felt. He was lovely to travel with.

On our last night together we went to the circus – it was quite an experience. Just watching the audience was enough entertainment! The men and boys in front of me and next to me shifted themselves nearer and nearer to me every time they thought Genaut was not looking!

I had a really nice trip to Darjeeling and some adventures on the way. When I was buying my ticket at the station, a young Indian man came up to help me. Next day when I left Varanasi, I saw him and his friends on the train. I was in the women's compartment but they were nearby and they came and sat with me for quite a lot of the journey and talked.

They were very nice types and looked after me completely as they were going the same way for most of the journey as far as Siliguri, after which they were taking a bus to Schillong, another hill station further east. The guy I had first met at the station invited me to stay in Schillong with a family that one of them knew. It would be nice but there are other places I would give priority to in India, as I do not have much time and also probably I would have to go around with him all the time. He was getting a bit possessive towards me and was saying he would like to go to England – they need a sponsor to do that. I shall have to write and thank them for helping me. We had to change trains mid-way and if it hadn't been for them I never would have had a seat – always there are so many crowds of people on Indian trains.

That journey took three days altogether. I slept on the train one night and the next night I wanted to sleep in the 'Retiring

Room' at Siliguri station before getting the toy train up the mountain in the early morning, but when I enquired I found that the Retiring Room had already been taken – it was a large room with two beds.

I went out of the station into the little town – primitive as always with its tatty market stalls, and I found two quite pleasant-looking hotels up the road. I pushed past the rickshaw drivers that approached me, as they do wherever you go. It's quite expensive to keep taking rickshaws.

I decided to stay in the second hotel. When the manager told me it was ten rupees, I said that was more than I wanted to pay. He was a young Sikh, quite good-looking. At once he said, "All right, you can have the room for eight rupees and I'll pay the other two out of my own pocket if you promise to stay here again on your way back."

I agreed at once that I would if I came back that way. Then he suggested that we have a drink together in my room but I was going to take a shower and I said I would come down to the restaurant afterwards. He at once said that was not possible as his parents were there and Sikhs are not allowed to drink! They had alcoholic drinks in this place for guests – unusual for India.

I asked him to wake me in the morning at 6 o'clock and he suggested coming at 5 o'clock! I said that was too early! Eventually he left to go home – worried that his parents would wonder where he was although he was well over twenty-one years. He said he owned the hotel but probably his father did.

It was so hot, but then there was a torrential rainstorm and the telegraph pole outside fell over. Sparks flew out dangerously and the lights kept going off. I had my shower and went down to drink a lassi in the restaurant. There, some guests (men) bought me a glass of wine. Afterwards they followed me to my room and I had to bolt them out! They get ideas here about Western girls from porn films and Western magazines.

I fell asleep for a couple of hours and woke up feeling so hot. The fan wasn't working. I went out to ask someone to fix it. There were a group of men standing around and one of them came to my room to see to it. I discovered that he was a manager from the hotel next door.

Within minutes he offered me free accommodation in his hotel where the fans "worked very well." I was just refusing when the manager from my hotel stepped into my small room and asked in English what "that man" was doing in my room! 'That man' answered him furiously, "What do you mean?" and the next second the first one punched him on the chin. They were both young Sikhs. There was a terrific scuffle as they both grappled with one another and I managed to shove them out of the room and bolt the door again. I could hear them fighting and shouting for over an hour after that in the corridor – they must have woken everyone in the hotel!

Next morning someone else, a hotel guest, that I had asked to wake me up, knocked on my door early, and I left the hotel to get on the little train at 7 o'clock. I was comfortably seated when the station master came up and asked me through the window whether I had a permit for Darjeeling. Of course I did not as I did not know one was needed. I was most annoyed that they had not told me before and I had been at the station an hour or so last night and also this morning. I had to get off the train and get a permit from the office. They were really nice to me though, and one of the ticket inspectors ordered me breakfast free of charge. He also demanded that I stay in the Retiring Room at the station for two nights on my return from Darjeeling. I again said 'yes' I would if I come back here (knowing that I most likely won't!).

I boarded the next train at 9.30, and was in a sweet little carriage with a nice family. The father was a doctor, and all the family – three girls – spoke perfect English, except their mother. The journey up the mountain took seven hours, as the train had to go very slowly. It was a little steam train, chugging along. The scenery was spectacular and so green and woody. Altogether we climbed 7000 feet.

Towards the end of the trip the weather changed and the sky was overcast. It started to pour with rain. I went with my Indian family to a lovely hotel – a Government approved Tourist Lodge right up high above the town. It used to be a Maharaja's palace and the people working there were nice – so genuine. In fact, I found a vast difference between the mountain people and those from the plains below, both in looks and in character. The mountain people are simple country people always ready to help anyone without any ideas of making a lot of money or taking advantage of lone female travellers! Or so it seemed. One day a little old man took me into a cafe and bought me tea and Indian sweets just for the sake of being friendly to foreigners, he said.

In the plains of India they are more worldly. At times their attitude towards me as a western woman has annoyed me very much – it is as though I am just an object of desire, and this is disrespectful. I feel that if they don't respect me then why should I have respect for them? However, when they buy me tea and snacks and meals I accept. Mostly, I am treated very kindly. The jeweller in the Clarks Shiraj Hotel in Agra bought me a lovely lunch even though I told him clearly that I was leaving that evening. (This was not the same jeweller who locked me in his shop and offered me an emerald ring!)

Now I want to carry on writing about my time in Darjeeling. The food at that Government Approved Lodge was fantastic and there was so much of it – delicious Indian curries. I paid 16.50 rupees a night (including two meals) which was cheap. The weather was quite cold, and every evening a boy who worked in the hotel brought a bundle of sticks up to the room and made a fire in the grate for me, as he did for all the guests. I stayed a couple of days there but then I moved to the youth hostel where there were more Europeans to talk to and it was cheaper. I ate out at the little restaurants with other travellers, especially two American girls I met who were travelling together.

The streets of Darjeeling are fun to walk around in – winding paths up and down steep mountain slopes, and a market. The town is on top of a mountain and the view is absolutely fantastic. Unfortunately there were mists and cloud most of the time which spoilt the view somewhat, so that I only saw the snow-capped peaks of the mountains opposite on one occasion. It is possible to see Mount Everest on a clear day. I visited 'The Mountaineering Institute' which is very interesting. It is like a museum and tells stories of all the mountaineers who have climbed Mount Everest.

I also visited two Buddhist monasteries in Darjeeling, containing many large Buddhas. Beneath the statues were many offerings: saucers of oil (butter lamps I think they are called), bowls of water, fruit, wheat and rice.

One morning I walked up to the monastery and saw monks with shaven heads – some young boys among them – making pyramid-shaped cakes out of soya flour from sacks sent by the charity Oxfam from abroad. These were being made for offerings in the temple. First of all I was disgusted, thinking that the cakes being offered would not be eaten, but afterwards I learned that next day was a holy day and then they would share the cakes out with people in the little village nearby which is a community of Tibetan refugees who have escaped from occupied Tibet (occupied by the Chinese). They were going to have the cakes blessed before sharing them out, which I think is a lovely idea.

I would have liked to talk to the monks as I have read much about the Buddhist religion especially when studying comparative religions at college, and it seems very beautiful and peace-loving to me, but I was not sure whether the monks could speak English or not, and perhaps they would not have spoken to me as a woman, so I did not get the chance.

However, later I visited The Tibetan Refugee Self-Help Centre – the little village a few kilometres away from the town in the mountains. It is a little communal settlement. The people there all work together making handicrafts to sell – there are carpentry shops where carpenters make carved, grotesque painted masks and furniture; work rooms for spinning and weaving carpets; rooms with cloth to make bags, shawls and belts – with gorgeous embroidery; and a painting workshop with beautiful watercolour paintings of Tibetan gods. There is a little shop from which tourists can buy, and the village has its own hospital, school and a little Buddhist temple. The people there look very happy. I saw the women dying rough wool with vegetable dyes – everything is done by hand and the children run around everywhere. There is a spectacular view from the village as it is at the top of the mountain, like Darjeeling. I like the Tibetan people so much. Some people there were able to speak a little English.

I also went to see the tea estate called Happy Valley in Darjeeling. It was pleasant walking along the tiny mountain paths through the estate – tea bushes everywhere as far as the eye can see. It is quite beautiful, and I saw women picking the tea in their colourful saris with great woven baskets on their backs. The factory is quite small and I saw the leaves being dried, sorted and sifted. There are nine different grades of tea. I was told that the first grade is export quality tea and is not drunk here at all. Probably most of the tea shops in Darjeeling use the ninth grade tea! I had a cup of chai at a little chai stall on the estate. The tea tasted the same as it does anywhere in India – tea, water, milk, spices and sugar all boiled together in a saucepan – it is far too sweet for me.

Darjeeling is so beautiful and the climate so much cooler, but in the winter it must get very cold. I think they have quite a lot of snow. Certainly there is always snow on the mountain peaks.

Chapter Eight
Calcutta – Bedbugs and Poverty

Monday, 3rd May 1976

It is impossible to keep up to date with all the news. Every minute of my time here is filled with interesting and exciting things – there is barely time to rest and drink it all in – let alone write about it all. That seems a waste of time. I don't have a second of my precious life to spare! Still, I will try!

At last I decided to leave Darjeeling even though I loved it there. I was tempted to go to Kathmandu but instead I decided to come back to the plains as I really want to see Calcutta and visit Mother Teresa's Homes, despite dreading the journey here. I travelled on the train by night again, after going by bus from Darjeeling part of the way down the mountain.

Once down in the plains, the air felt hot and stifling again. Urban India thrust its ugly face at us (or so it seemed to me after the Himalayas) and a feeling of depression swept through me and apparently through the others in my carriage too. For the umpteenth time I thought to myself, 'How I hate India with its dirt and its slums, its beggars and its stifling heat'. And yet, how strange – after a while the country seems to seep into my veins and become part of me, so that I feel a wild love for it, fed by a hunger of mine to see it and know it and live it… Because India really is an experience to live: so different, so fascinating, so strange, so incredible, I could sit and watch the movements and activities of the many, many people in the streets hour after hour, day after day, and never get bored. There is so much going on.

I could say right now, truthfully, 'I love India' and yet sometimes I loathe it too. I know I am not alone in feeling like this. I have met people who are disillusioned with India, but most people are fascinated by it, and everybody agrees that it is necessary to stay here for a period of time to try to understand the country, to slow down into the pace of life and grow into it and learn about the life of the people – it is so very different from anything anybody could experience anywhere in the West. How I wish I had more time. I would like to stay longer in each place, but I am anxious to see too much – as always.

When I arrived in Calcutta this morning, I took a rickshaw with an American girl who is also going to stay here a few days. The rickshaws are all pulled by hand here – not bicycle. It is humiliating to be pulled along in a little carriage by a man or boy running as often as not barefoot along the stony, dirty streets of the city. I feel that if they can walk it, then I can too. Since that first ride I have wanted to avoid taking rickshaws here – I would rather travel on the trams and buses, they are much cheaper anyway. There are thousands of rickshaw drivers that bother you on every street corner. I feel sorry for them though. I suppose they can't afford bicycle rickshaws.

The buildings in Calcutta look dilapidated. As we were going through the city I saw many that look as though they need renovating or to be pulled down and completely rebuilt. We went to the Salvation Army guest house, which we heard is about the cleanest and cheapest place in town – eleven rupees a night with breakfast – still pretty expensive compared with prices of guest houses in smaller towns.

When I arrived there with the American girl, we were told

that tonight there is only one vacancy, so I left and let her have it. I went down the road and have found the Paragon Hotel where I am now staying. It is only six rupees a night.

As I said before, my special aim in coming to Calcutta is to see Mother Teresa's homes. I feel too that as Calcutta is so famous (or infamous) for its poverty and its slums, I ought to see it. It was once the capital of India – when the British were here.

As soon as I arrived here, I dumped my rucksack and my carrier bag of books that is my luggage, in the Paragon Hotel, and set off to find Mother Teresa's 'Home for the Dying and Destitute'. I spoke to someone who has been there and she told me where it is, warning me about the area which is very poor and depressing and unsafe to walk around in alone. She advised me not to go alone but to wait until someone else wanted to go, but I felt that I might have to wait several days for that, so I went alone in a taxi.

The area is indeed very poor and depressing with dirty stalls and barrows selling things everywhere and people mooning around in the heat. So many beggars came up to me as I got out of the taxi, that I gave to no one – otherwise I knew I would be surrounded. In other parts of Calcutta when coming from the station, I did not see so many beggars as this, and it is possible to give a few paisa without others approaching. I have been told that the city has been cleaned up in the last year and many beggars transported to the country villages where hopefully they will be better off – but possibly they came to Calcutta from the country in the first place to try to find work. Calcutta is so crowded.

When I arrived at the gate of the Home for the Dying and Destitute, I found it to be barred, but an Indian boy let me in when I knocked. He said it was closed to keep the place cool and because the Sisters (nuns) had just left for their afternoon break. It was just after noon. I went inside and was told that the nuns would be returning at about half past three.

There was a large hall with low simple beds, dormitory style and there were many fans. The place had a peaceful atmosphere even though it was depressing. Many of the men lying on the beds (this first room was the men's ward) were like living skeletons. I did not feel repelled by the sight but I did feel pity. However, at least they are inside in this cooler place away from the heat and the dirt and the flies.

The room was clean and on the walls were Bible quotations and prayers – like I have seen in Catholic homes – and there was a statue of the Virgin Mary and a picture of Mother Teresa. As the patients must all be Hindus, I wondered if it is a bit inappropriate. However, I know that Hindus think of Jesus as another god, or a holy man. Hindus also have their own charitable organisations, sometimes with pictures of Indian gurus on the wall.

Some of the patients were not thin and some were sitting up and conversing with their neighbours. There were no blankets of course as it is far too hot. When I was not standing directly under a fan, I still poured sweat, but we English of course suffer far more from the heat than Indians do.

I went into the women's ward next door. Whereas most of the men wore loin cloths, some of the women and girls wore simple cotton frocks. I was told later that these are sent from abroad and altered by the women using sewing machines.

I was disappointed that the nuns were not there for me to speak to. The two boy workers spoke a little English and told me it would be a good idea to go to 'Mother House' to speak to the Sisters there. They described to me how to get there by tram and bus. But I decided that I was going to wait until they came and I went outside and walked around the area, but I didn't stay out for more than ten minutes in that midday heat. One small boy came up and beckoned to me to come and see the temple nearby, which I did. It was the temple of the goddess Kali where they have animal sacrifices – how horrible! There were so many beggars and pathetic-looking people around – some looked as though they suffered with stunted growth. When I see places like this in India, I wonder how the human race can get itself into such a terrible state.

A pack of wild-looking stray dogs, howling and showing their teeth, sent me back quickly to the shelter of the home. It is possible that some of them could have rabies, especially in this area. I have heard of several people who have been bitten by dogs in India. Some of the local people were laughing as I ran away from them. I did not make my fear of these dogs any secret! Many animals in India are so lean and desperate-looking. The cats here make our western cats seem dopey and lazy as they have an air of great alertness; their necks and ears appear to be longer as they look all around them and their faces have a different expression and are much bonier and more protruding. Some dogs in some places are friendly to humans and wag their tails, but I did not see any like that here.

I went back into the home for a while, and then decided to go out and try to find 'Mother House'. I thought it would be interesting to see where the nuns lived, but it might have been better to stay and wait for them to come back, because I spent the whole afternoon going on buses and trams around Calcutta looking for the place.

There are actually very few cars or taxis in Calcutta. The streets are crowded with bicycles, pedestrians, rickshaws and animals, especially cows, walking in the streets. The buses and trams are crammed full of people actually hanging out of the entrances holding on for dear life, sometimes on the rooftops too, just as I have seen them do on trains. It is almost impossible to squeeze in but they do still squash more people in at every stop.

The sight of a bus going by is like watching a comic film, but it is not so funny trying to get on one. There is a bus conductor inside who seems to manage to get everyone's fare – at least I did not get away without paying the twenty paisa (about 2p) but perhaps that is because I was noticed, being European. People sit on the large wire luggage racks on the roof. I think it is cooler for them than sitting inside the bus. On some buses you can see so many people up there that it appears that they are falling over the sides! When I was travelling through Pakistan I used to try to avoid putting my pack on top. If you have luggage up there you have to watch that nothing is stolen out of it.

I thought I was going to 'Mother House' but somebody directed me to the wrong place with the same name and I ended up at about half past four, very tired, at a nursing home! I climbed some stairs and went into a room where I saw some girls sitting. They happened to be a family sitting in their private home! They were so pleased to see me, told me to sit down and chattered away, but I was so tired I could barely bring myself to be sociable. (Last night I was travelling all night on the train!) They invited me to their sister's wedding next Sunday and I said I will go if I am still in Calcutta!

I went across to the school opposite to enquire where Mother House was, but really I just wanted to get back to my hotel and sleep. The Indian girl and her younger sister came on the bus with me most of the way, and then she insisted on buying me a drink in a restaurant. People are so nice to me here but I never did find 'Mother House.'

Tuesday, 4th May 1976

Finally I got back to the hotel last night, longing for a good night's sleep but it was not to be! In the Paragon Hotel there were many low beds with mattresses squashed together in one room. I looked at the mattress I had been allocated and saw that there were what looked like bed-bug eggs on the bed. (I have seen them before!) I decided to take another bed in the room and I lay down on it but it was really hot and I couldn't sleep. The manager then came up to me and told me I was sleeping in somebody else's bed, so I told him there were bed bugs in my bed and I refused to move. He made some excuse that they could not get new mattresses. Then he whispered, "You can come and sleep with me in my bed if you like – I have clean mattress." Typical – he knew I was alone!

 I slept on my bed in the Paragon for an hour and then I woke up and felt myself being bitten by bed-bugs, and I saw some live ones crawling on the bed – they are small, round, flat, red, beetle-like creatures – awful! I went and lay on the floor in between the beds although I was squashed like a sardine. I imagined that all the bugs were coming down at me from all the beds around about, and they probably were because they often live in the wood of the furniture and can smell you. In my frustration I got up and went outside in the courtyard – it was about one o'clock in the morning – where people were still sitting chatting. I found a high metal counter in the corridor where I lay my sleeping bag and climbed up. I had been going to sleep on the ground but somebody pointed out the 'shrews' as they called them. They looked more like rats scuttling about to me. I spent a more restful, but hot night on that counter.

 Before I went to sleep I saw a little man moving about. In the morning I was told by somebody that he usually slept up on that counter – that was his bed! He was one of the workers or managers in the hotel – but he never told me to get down so I stayed up there.

I have heard that in Calcutta there are religious people who pay passers-by to sleep on mattresses in the open air for the night – mattresses full of bed-bugs! They do it to feed the bed-bugs as a religious act of charity! In Hinduism all living creatures have souls. (I also believe that – but I would not give my body to feed bed-bugs!) There are also temples in India where rats are fed, and other temples where monkeys are fed.

When I woke up this morning I met a girl called Harriet who is also staying at the same hotel, and we went to eat breakfast together at a cafe down the road – rice, chapattis and curry. I told Harriet about my experience in the night and that I wanted to move my things to the Salvation Army guest house if they now had a vacancy for me, because I heard that it is at least clean and cooler. Harriet said she was not going to bother to move as she did not think there were any bed-bugs in her bed. Perhaps she is just lucky, although I doubt it very much as all the beds are squashed close together. I think she must be a heavy sleeper! Anyway, I could not stand to stay there for one more night!

It is so hot in Calcutta that I pour sweat all the time night and day, but I have made some nice friends here – girls for a change. Harriet I particularly like. She also is travelling alone. She is from Rhodesia, but she told me she worked as an agency nurse in London for a long time to earn her money for travelling. She said she is going east from Calcutta to Thailand and then travelling on to Australia, as was the American girl and so many others I have met. It sounds wonderful. Perhaps next time I might do this!

Harriet is very well-spoken, very charming, lady-like and quite conventional in her way. I feel at home in her company and I realise that often I get on far better with conventional people even though I am not really conventional myself! Harriet eats in the cheapest of places. I have found that English people I have met always live much more cheaply than Germans or Americans – perhaps the latter have more money than us!

Harriet and I went to the cinema together this evening to see 'Siddhartha' – the film of a book by Herman Hesse which I love. The price of the cinema was 3 rupees 90 paisa. I really enjoyed the film.

Over breakfast, I told Harriet about the manager of the Paragon Hotel coming to me in the night and inviting me into his bed. I don't think Harriet has so much trouble with propositions from men as I do – perhaps I just look the type who would sleep around! I am not though! Twice I have been asked, "Do you belong to the hippy community?" That really annoys me because they call all European travellers 'hippies', and most travellers I have met are extremely well-educated with university degrees, if they aren't students taking a year off from their studies. I have also met so many ex-teachers, and almost all western women wear long skirts because they are more practical here – both because Indian women wear them (saris), and to save their legs being bitten by mosquitoes. I wear my long wrap-around skirt and either a white T-shirt or the black sari top which I bought. I love wearing that.

Harriet told me she also wanted to see Mother Teresa's homes, so I moved my things to the Salvation Army hostel where I am now staying, and here we asked for proper directions for visiting Mother Teresa's Children's Home for Destitute Babies, which happens to be within walking distance. This time some of the nuns were there. They wear white cotton saris edged with blue and are much more informally dressed than western nuns. They happen to be all Indian nuns but can speak English and are very sweet. They talked a lot to us about the babies – so tiny they were, all lying in cots – some very thin. Many have been brought in off the streets, abandoned by their parents probably because they were too poor to support them. The children range in age from nought years to about six. The older ones looked happy and laughed a lot, flinging their arms around us. I stayed till midday and helped feed the babies. The nuns told us that Mother Teresa is at present in America.

I think the home is wonderful, but I have heard that Mother Teresa will not allow anybody to adopt the children unless they are Roman Catholic Christians. I think this is a shame because otherwise they might be adopted by good Hindu families. Obviously the children must all have originally come from Hindu families, but at the home they all have to convert to Catholicism which seems wrong. It made me wonder whether Mother Teresa would do this charity work at all if she were not allowed to convert people! Imagine an orphanage in England where all the children are forced to convert to Hinduism and Christian families are not allowed to adopt them at all! This would not be allowed!

In India people are very tolerant and acknowledge all religions. The Indian Government is trying to encourage birth control as India's population is growing so fast – it is said that in the year 2000 there will be a billion people in India. Mother Teresa endorses the view of the Catholic Church that birth control is against the will of God. There is nothing in the Bible that I have ever read that says this. I wonder why church leaders have such strong views about things like this. It seems to me that birth control is the only thing that can save India from so much poverty. It is so terrible for women who are already so poor to keep having babies that they cannot support.

Of course, the Salvation Army are also doing good work among the poor in Calcutta – with the same idea of also hoping to convert people to Christianity! The guest house is called Red Shield Hostel. It is at least clean and they serve big breakfasts in the comfortable, though Spartan-looking lounge, even though it is quite expensive here. It is run by a middle-aged English woman who seems to be somewhat neurotic, over-fussy and conservative. When I arrived she was scolding one boy for going into the girls' dormitory. In this Christian-run mission hostel, this is strictly forbidden. I think he only went in there to talk to his girlfriend. She even pointed at me on the other side of the room, when talking to the boy, saying that as a girl alone, I would not like the idea of a boy going into my dormitory! It would not bother me at all, but I didn't say anything. In most places there are no restrictions like that.

I was very surprised when I found out later today that she is married to a dark-skinned Indian – also a member of the Salvation Army – who looks quite a bit younger than her. She has a dark-skinned teenage daughter and I heard her shouting at her, forbidding her to do something. In some ways she seems so typically English to me; perhaps it is just the English accent that is so familiar to me – I rarely hear it here. She is nice to me but I feel sorry for her daughter as her mother seems to be constantly nagging her.

After we returned from Mother Teresa's children's home, I was told at the guest house about a 'feeding centre' set up by the Salvation Army in Calcutta, so I went there later this afternoon to see it. It is run by a certain Major Gardener, a retired Major from the Indian army at the time of the British, and I found out that he is as famous as Mother Teresa in Calcutta, and a film has been made about him, showing his feeding programme for the poor which he operates all alone.

He is an enormous fat man with a beard – not fat because he overeats I am sure, as he says he eats only once a day. But he has a disease which has caused his legs to swell up terribly and he can only walk very slowly as they are completely bandaged.

I felt really honoured to meet him. He is one of those characters you can never forget – like a kind of Santa Claus. He was very friendly to me but when I first arrived he said to me, "You have come just at the wrong time, as I'm just about to start feeding people."

Actually it was just the right time. I saw a lot of poor people come into the large hall, queue up and receive large helpings of the soupy curry from enormous pots on the stove. The Major called me over to talk to him while he was dishing it out. Some mothers received large bowls of food for their whole family. The soup was very thick, containing vegetables, chicken, wheat, vitamins, etc.

Afterwards the Major said I can go out with him in the van on Thursday evening when he takes out food to feed the people in the slums. In anticipation of this, I have booked my train ticket for Puri, the next step of my journey, for Friday night.

Friday, 7th May 1976

On Wednesday I walked around Calcutta all day. I spent hours wandering around one fascinating market nearby, bargaining but buying very little. There are many cheap restaurants in Calcutta. Nearly every restaurant is an open air restaurant full of people, and there are street stalls selling food everywhere. There are barrows full of green coconuts. When you buy one, the stall holder chops the top off and makes a hole in the top so that a straw can be placed in it and you can drink the creamy coconut water inside. It is delicious and very good for health. These coconuts cost 75 paisa (about 4 pence). There are also stalls selling freshly-squeezed fruit juice – pineapple and orange – with ice for one or two rupees. I am a bit dubious about drinking from these stalls. They have only one or two glasses which they wash in a bucket of water under the counter. It does not always look clean and the ice cannot be drinking water either, but I get so thirsty in the heat that sometimes that I take the risk. Luckily I have not been sick again.

Cows and bullocks wander around the streets as they do in all Indian towns, eating anything they can find, sometimes off the stalls. There are many curd and lassi shops. The lassi in Calcutta is especially delicious, and the restaurants seem cleaner than in the country towns so I don't mind eating in cheap places here. I have been very, very lucky – I have had no more stomach trouble at all – so far!

However, the muscles of my left leg have become painful because I have been doing too much walking after I sprained my ankle. I have not rested it enough! Finally my leg refused to go any further and I was forced to rest it most of yesterday morning and afternoon before going out in the evening. I had to force myself to stay in the hotel. I can't bear to waste a moment here. Most of the time I have one little thing wrong with me at a time. I had a septic thumb for a while which was really painful. I merely pricked my finger when I was darning a small hole in my skirt. I must have got an infection in my thumb. You have to be so careful with minor cuts and abrasions here as the streets are so dirty.

I have met so many travellers with infected wounds and even boils, as well as amoebic dysentery. One westerner I met had a swollen foot which he said had begun as a tiny heady spot – perhaps it was a mosquito bite. Wounds on feet are quite dangerous. I took the utmost care of my infected thumb – I bought antiseptic cream, bandaged it, and when the pain went away, I broke the skin of the swelling and let out the pus inside. It had swelled up quite a lot. After that and with regular cleaning, my thumb healed up quite quickly.

In one street, I saw Paul, a boy from Bath whom I had met on the Magic Bus. It was a nice surprise to run into him in a cafe. How sun-tanned he is.

Going out with the Major yesterday, Thursday evening, was an experience I will never forget. When I arrived, some of his helpers were playing draughts, and then later, when he came and before we went out, he made me a cup of very sweet tea and got out a large tin of biscuits, urging me to help myself. Then he said to me, "Tell me about yourself."

Somehow I felt shy with him, but then I feel shy with everyone. He is such a kind man. He introduced me to his 'sons', two adopted Indian boys who live with him in the hostel where he lives. They helped him carry the huge pots of food out to the van. On the way we collected more food left out by the canteen of some office blocks, and then went on to the slum areas.

The van stopped in about six different areas altogether and each time small groups of poor people queued up with their cards. The Major cannot feed everyone – as it is he feeds six thousand people per day and the cost is eight hundred rupees per day which is supplied entirely by voluntary donations. A social worker goes out to check on the most needy people – 'eligible' people are mothers with large families, old people, and those who cannot work. I watched from the van as the people took the food to their little street corners and sat on the pavement sharing it out. On one occasion a little boy climbed up into the van and Major Gardener picked him up in his arms. The people were very happy because there was more food that evening – one office canteen had left out a great pot of rice, and apparently rice is rationed in India.

Eventually the trip was finished; just one evening's work out of all those evenings in nineteen years since the day when the Major, who must be over sixty-five years, walked into the Salvation Army headquarters and asked if they had any work for him. He is not paid for his work but lives off his pension with which he also educates young Indian boys. The lady who runs the Salvation Army hostel told me this. He wears very loose white cotton clothes – much like Indian men wear. When they dropped me back at the hostel later, the Major told me to come back and visit them on my way back to Calcutta, which I would do if I returned this way. Everybody I meet asks me to visit them again on my way back!

It is wonderful what the Major is doing, but how terrible that people are living in such conditions and such poverty as this in Calcutta. The government of India needs to do something about it – needs to care. I feel that the caste system is at fault. Calcutta should not be like this, like a hell hole. How did it get like this? Hundreds of years ago I bet it was different – more countryside, trees perhaps, and far, far less people: that is the secret.

I wonder whether the Major is a lonely man – but perhaps not. He seems to own nothing and has no real family here –

his life is his work, but I think he is fulfilled. He told me he is looking for somebody to carry on his work when he is gone. I wonder if his sons will do it. I had the feeling that he was thinking of me. At one time I had thought that perhaps I could stay and do charity work in Calcutta, but Calcutta is such a terrible place. It depresses me so much that I know I can't stay here long. It is not my destiny and I am restless to go on travelling further.

Even though I am religious – I believe in all religions – I don't believe in missionaries. I don't believe that people should try to convert others. It is beautiful to help others, but for their sake only; not to change their religion — that is aggression. I do not feel that Major Gardener is doing his wonderful work for the wrong reasons though. I feel that he genuinely wants to give of his love, although I suppose his religion influences him, as Mother Teresa's does. There is nothing wrong in this. Whatever influences us to do something beautiful is good, as long as our ideas are not forced on others.

Chapter Nine
Puri and Hindu Temples

Tuesday, 11th May 1976

I am now in Puri, a little market town on the north-east coast. I have so much to write about. It is slow and peaceful here with its golden beach – so different from Calcutta – and it is refreshingly cool by the sea. But my time in Calcutta was very interesting. When the time came, I was even quite sorry to leave the city with its bustle of life and many markets.

I have had a lovely time here in Puri. My ankle is also much better now. Right now I am sitting in Santana's restaurant near the beach. It is a lovely friendly little place and I have just had breakfast. Every few minutes I stop writing and chat to people here – young Europeans and some American travellers. I don't mind sitting here inside, because the mornings are so hot. It seems to cool down in the afternoon. Some of the other travellers are sitting here reading too. The sweet peanut and coconut balls are really delicious. They are handmade and are sold in large glass jars in the shops.

I have so much to write about the three days that I have spent in Puri that I don't know where to begin, or whether to start now or write in here later, but as it is still early and too hot to go out, I think I shall stay here in this cafe and write now.

The journey from Calcutta to Puri took twelve hours. I very nearly missed the train as I went out to eat with Harriet and my room-mate first, and then caught the tram to the station. Of course the tram was jam-packed as usual and then a terrific rainstorm began and traffic everywhere was held up. I was on that tram for about an hour and then had to squeeze out with my haversack. At least the rainfall brought the temperature down in Calcutta. I read in the newspaper afterwards that they had two inches of rain in two hours and there were floods in Park Street. The streets all have English names – so much is written in English in India. I arrived at the station two minutes before my train went and was helped again by a really nice man who found my carriage for me.

Again I was in the women's carriage but this time it was a drag. It was the only compartment in the carriage with a sliding door which cut it off from the corridor and one lady in there said she had just recovered from measles so she wanted the windows and shutters closed all night. She was very nice to me, offering me chocolate and telling me to inform her if I needed anything in the night, and so I didn't have the heart to complain about the windows at first, but it was so stiflingly hot. Worst of all I suffered from claustrophobia being shut up in that small, hot carriage, and eventually I got up in the night and opened the window.

Finally I arrived in Puri and I got a rickshaw to the youth hostel, a beautiful new building right on the golden beach. The address of it was in my guide book. The youth hostels in India do seem to be very nice. Most of them are quite new. Here I have met two American girls that I made friends with in Darjeeling. They missed out Calcutta having been there before.

Puri is a lovely place, full of Hindu temples. Unfortunately, non-Hindus are not allowed inside, but the outsides are interesting enough with huge domes and carvings and bright paintings of the gods. Very often it is possible to see inside the entrance. The idols here are so primitive-looking and sometimes look like brightly painted dolls or papier-mache models – like those made in English primary schools!

Here in Puri the most famous temple is that of Lord Jaganath – a god with a face that looks as though the features were drawn by a young child. He has a mouth which is a line turned up into a smile. He sits with two other gods, a small one being in the middle. I must find out more about this god. The Hindu religion is fascinating and very symbolic. I know that in Hindu philosophy the many gods are supposed to be symbols of the many facets of personality of a supreme God or Divine Spirit over all, but many of the ordinary people take them literally and worship the idols. In Hinduism, all beliefs are accepted because God, the Divine, is omnipresent and omnipotent. He is everywhere, in everything, and can take on any form.

I have been swimming in the sea here but it is very rough which is a pity. I have also been a couple of times to the huge market square where the large temple is. The market here is the most fascinating that I have yet seen in India, with its many handicrafts so beautifully made. I wish I had money to buy more.

Yesterday I was talking to a middle-aged Indian man while I was on the beach. I told him I would like to see inside the Hindu temples where non-Hindus are not allowed to go, so he told me he would take me inside one of the temples as his converted Hindu wife. He said the priest would allow me if I was with him. I got dressed and put a scarf over my head and we went into one of the temples. We had to take our shoes off at the entrance as you always do in holy places in India. I was so excited to be able to go into the inner sanctuary. Inside there was a man beating a drum and an elephant.

When we came out, my friend invited me to lunch at his hotel, saying he was alone and merely wanted company. First of all I was dubious but he was so insistent that at last I agreed. I enjoyed the meal and we chatted in his room. Afterwards, when I could see that he might get a bit randy, I made the excuse that I wanted to go to the market. He was leaving by the afternoon train which was the only reason why I agreed to have lunch with him!

He at once said he would come to the market with me on his way to the station. He took his luggage with him in the rickshaw. When we arrived at the market he started buying me lots of presents in spite of my protests. However, I finally accepted them. He told me how much pleasure I had given him just talking to him that afternoon. He bought a little stone statue of a god for me, and then straw mats, a basket and some bangles.

When I went to buy a couple of wooden toys that I thought I might send to my nephew, he paid for them. Probably I won't send them – they are so heavy, but it was a lovely thought. He would have bought more for me but there wasn't time anyway and I ushered him away to the station where I insisted on buying him a cup of tea (30 paisa). There I saw him off. I must say, I am glad he didn't stay longer. I would have felt obliged to spend more time with him as he had given me so many presents. He gave me his address in Amritsar but of course I shan't go and stay there!

After that I returned to the market place where I got pestered by many young boys, one who stayed with me all evening showing me around. There is a festival going on here for a few days and we are in the middle of it. Every evening from one of the temples they carry some of the gods high on platforms covered with flowers, rice and fruits. I stayed to watch this last night. It was fascinating. The streets were crowded with people – pilgrims, tourists and street sellers selling balloons, flutes, snake skins, handmade drums, all kinds of foods and sweets, and a thousand other things.

I walked through the streets until I came to the Water Temple, a brightly painted temple in the middle of a large square moat surrounded by concrete steps. It is quite common for temples to be surrounded by a moat in India – I have seen it before. Many young boys in loin cloths were swimming in the moat and diving off the temple walls. The area became crowded and at eight o'clock the 'chariots' of gods were carried through the streets followed by a man riding an elephant that lives in one of the temples. It might have been the one I saw in the afternoon. It was adorned with rich colourful cloths and flowers and looked so beautiful. What a gorgeous creature it was – I love elephants. I wonder if it is happy living there. I hope so. I would prefer to see elephants living free in the wild with their families.

The flowers and petals surrounding the idols lying on the platforms were given away to the people in the crowds and the gods were taken on two boats decked out with flowers and floated around the temple amid cheers from the crowds standing and sitting around watching. The temple was lit up and so were the many palm trees around it on the other side. It was quite a spectacle.

Because I was the only westerner around last evening, Indians stood around me in a circle gaping at me. I seemed to be the second attraction — the first one being the gods in their chariots! When I bought some bananas, I turned around to see a whole crowd of young boys curiously following me! One of them, who had spoken to me previously, started leading me around. I sat down with him on a bench to await the coming of the chariots and was surrounded by about twelve boys of all ages, the youngest being six or seven, merely standing gaping at me in silence as though I was a lifeless model! When I laughed and poked at them in fun they smiled but otherwise were perfectly serious. It was so funny. At last I bought the three smallest boys (all about six years old) a balloon each, and they smiled and turned away. That broke up the party!

I wish I could have seen some westerners at the festival. I did not see one, although I know there are quite a few of us staying here in Puri. At last I walked back in the evening and returned to the house on the beach where I am now staying with some other westerners.

Yesterday I had to move out of the youth hostel because it was fully booked with a party of people, and I was invited to stay in this house on the beach. The room here costs only one and a half rupees a night. It is merely a large stone shelter with archways and steps. We slept on the platform facing the beach last night. There was a breeze but it was still hot and sticky, and I missed not having a cool shower – still, it was all right. This morning I came here to this cafe with the other people to have breakfast and drink coffee, and that is where I am now writing this diary.

Some westerners here smoke marijuana or take illegal drugs. One woman here asked me if I would like to take some with her, but I refused because I know how dangerous they are. After trying marijuana once in Amsterdam, I have made a vow to myself that I will never take drugs again. I am so glad I made that decision. Who knows what could happen to me here? I take so many other kinds of risks as it is!

Madras

Wednesday, 19th May 1976

I am now on my way down south to the ferry where I can get the boat across from India to Jaffna in Sri Lanka. I have heard that the mangoes are wonderful there. I have a large gap to fill in about my adventures after leaving Puri. I want to write about Madras in south India because I had an eventful time there.

I travelled on the train from Puri with a Swiss guy whom I met at the station. Towards the end of the journey which took about thirty-six hours, I started talking to an Indian man sitting in the same compartment. He invited me to stay a couple of nights with him and his wife and family, saying he would take me to visit an Indian classical dance school. As it was already evening, I decided to take a chance and go and stay there – I could always leave if I suspected trouble! We took the bus in Madras and arrived at his house – a pleasant, 'middle-class' (I hate that term) home in a nice area. His home was actually a top apartment in a two storey house. Below his flat was a doctor's surgery. His wife – a typical, sweet, docile-looking lady in a sari – came to the door and I met his daughter, a fifteen-year-old girl also in a sari, and his eleven-year-old son.

The family welcomed me heartily, although only the husband could speak English. The son and daughter spoke a little broken English which they had learned at school, but they were very shy.

The wife set out banana leaves as plates on the floor of the dining room and brought in a meal that she had cooked. It was rice and curry of course, with some vegetables – all very spicy. I have discovered that south Indian food is spicier than the traditional food of northern India. The curry was made with a coconut-based sauce – very delicious. They eat rice instead of chapattis. The family sat cross-legged on the floor, and invited me to sit with them. We all ate with our fingers. They were genuinely interested in me, but of course, as always, the usual question came up: "Are you alone?"

The daughter said in her language, Tamil: "She should come with her parents." I told them that my parents did not want to travel. The husband translated. I know they disapprove of women travelling alone, but anyway, they were still very nice to me.

I tucked in straight away with the husband and son and then realised that we were the only ones eating. The wife and daughter sat and watched us. When I asked why they were not eating, I was told that it is customary for the wife to wait until after her husband has finished his meal and she will usually serve him with several helpings of rice and curry. By that time I saw that the food was cold! Later, during other meals, sometimes the daughter would eat with us (but I felt that that was just for my sake) and at other times she would wait for her mother.

During my stay in that house, the husband wanted to take me around – too much! First he took me to Madras beach in the evening. There were many stalls and stall holders selling their wares on the beach.

The husband told me he owns some rice fields, and rents out some property. Also, he said he has been a journalist and has written and published a book that is going to be made into a film in Tamil. He said he would invite me to act in it when the time comes. I take everything people say to me here with a pinch of salt! He was an interesting character but I could see that he was taking too much interest in me as a woman, and I suspected that it was not a rare thing for him to be unfaithful to his wife when he is away from home. In fact, he told me that he would be if the opportunity came his way, and I found out, none too soon, that he hoped to have the opportunity with me – even with his wife there! That to me, reflects the Indian husband's attitude towards women – that they are the passive, docile, less important sex.

After I went to the beach with him, I made the decision that I would not go anywhere else with him alone. I told the husband that if he wanted the sort of payment that I was not prepared to give, then I had better leave then and there and find somewhere else to stay. He would not hear of that. He asked me if I would contact some Indian shops in London for him, give them his card, and ask if they would like a business arrangement with him. He said he could send handicrafts to shops there and I would get a cut of the profit. However, I know that there are so many Indians living in England who are already importing things from India.

That night and the other nights I was there, I slept in the sitting room with the two children. The daughter slept on a bed and the son slept on a mat on the floor. I also slept on my sleeping bag on a mat on the floor. In the morning, the wife presented me with the most delicious cup of south Indian coffee I have ever tasted, and probably ever will.

The next morning I went to book my train ticket for the next lap of my journey. The son seemed to like me and accompanied me there, but I discovered that there was no train for another two days. The family insisted that I stay with them for the next three nights until my train journey.

The husband took me to visit a dance school as he had promised. I watched a class of girls learning the classical dances – it was so beautiful. The husband suggested that I could learn Indian dance at the school and stay with his family in their house. I would love to learn Indian classical dance, but now is not the right time for me, as I am going back to college in England in September to finish my university degree course.

In the afternoon I went sight-seeing and shopping for lungies to sell in Sri Lanka, as some travellers have advised me to take lungies and saris there to sell for a profit. I have decided to try it just for fun.

It was lovely staying with the family, but the husband started to bring up the subject of sex with me more and more, discussing the difference in attitudes between East and West. He even did this in front of his family, knowing they could not understand. He told me of another English girl who had stayed with them. Later, when I asked him, he told me she had slept with him. I wondered if she had felt obliged to, in return for her food and lodging. He was not going to cajole me into doing that! I offered to pay him money for letting me stay there but he would not take any. He said to me, "That's not what I want from you but you won't give me what I really want."

In the husband's eyes, he was doing nothing wrong in making sexual advances to me – but what is right and wrong anyway, and mere custom? I did not approve of it since he had such a sweet wife and lovely family, but then they also disapproved of me as a lone woman traveller, yet they still accepted me as I am. So in the same way I accept these people for their attitudes, some of which I dislike.

The husband saw himself as lord of his house. He was a Hindu, but Muslims have many wives and are not faithful to just one woman. He told me that his wife knew that he liked young girls and accepted the fact that he might sleep with one if he were away from home. He told me that if I liked, he would get his wife's permission to sleep with me. He said she would give it. I said, "Yes, but she would not be very happy, would she?" He agreed on that but the idea did not upset him much. It would be easier all round to do the thing without telling her. "We could go in the other room at night," he said. "It would be easy."

I laughed it all off as a joke, but I said to him, "If my husband did that I'd divorce him. I would not put up with it." He said, "I know you would, but my wife could not do that to me."

I told him I would never have any relationship with him as a married man on principle, for his wife's sake. I told him I hated the Indian attitude of men towards women as second-class citizens who are inferior. I said that for me, men and women are equal. I even said that his wife was too good for him. He said to me while she was standing there, "Look at my wife, she's like a rhinoceros."

She was on the plump side even though she must only have been in her early thirties. The wife smiled sweetly when he said that, as if she understood. Good thing she didn't! I said to him, "You have a very nice wife." Sometimes I wondered if the children understood anything or suspected but they all acted as if they liked me very much.

I tried to show my gratitude to them for letting me stay there, by buying a little thing each day for the family, like fruit or sweets.

My reason for coming to Madras was to visit a poor Indian boy of twelve years who lives with his family in a thatched hut in a fishermen's village on a beach near Madras. I have sponsored him for the last two years with an organisation, paying a few pounds a year to help with his education. While in Madras, I contacted the office there to find out where the family live so that I could go and see them. A woman working in the office gave me directions, so I set out on the bus to find them. I asked what the family would like as a gift and she suggested plantains (bananas). Bananas are so cheap here. I was surprised but I realised later that she must have suggested that because they are cheap, just to be polite.

I bought some bananas because I thought she was serious, but I also bought the boy a T-shirt. The boy has several brothers and sisters and I met them all. They and the parents all live in the two roomed hut together – it is made of woven palm leaves. The hut village is scruffy-looking. His father was a fisherman but he has been injured in an accident. His mother cooks on a tiny stove inside the hut. They all seemed to be so nervous of me. Perhaps they have never met anybody from Europe before. I took the boy out and bought him an ice cream. It was a lovely experience to meet him and his family. I am glad I have been able to help them a little, although I feel that my small amount of money cannot do much. They all need sponsors.

Afterwards I went back to the house of my other Indian family as they insisted that I stay there. On the night before the last, the husband woke me up in the middle of the night. I told him sharply to leave me alone and he went back to bed. I was considering leaving the next day but my train was booked for the morning after. I was to have only one more night there. It did not seem worth the bother of looking around for a new place to stay for one night, and anyway, the rest of the family would wonder why I was leaving suddenly when they knew the date for which I had booked the train journey.

On the very last night the husband was really troublesome. I think probably I had not sounded fierce enough in my rejection of him before, but I find it hard to show aggression to people by raising my voice. He would not leave me in peace there on the floor. I was afraid his children would wake up. At last I threatened to get up and tell his wife, and when I got up to do it, he eventually went back to bed and left me to sleep. Next day he was friendly towards me as though nothing had happened, and urged me to stay there again when I return from Sri Lanka – which I shall not!

On the last day I bought them a bottle of mango juice which the children like and I took their son with me to the swimming pool and bought him a drink there. I had bought them small presents every day, but the mother said I had bought too much. I hoped I had not offended them. She went out and bought me a set of gold coloured bangles and a necklace. The daughter bought me a string of sweet-smelling flowers (jasmine, I think) for my hair. This is a lovely south Indian custom – to wear flowers in your hair – all the women do it. There are so many street sellers selling blossoms on chains with pink and white flowers. They have such a wonderful perfume.

When it was time to leave, the husband called a rickshaw to take me to the station as he was going that way. He insisted on paying. He said to me, "Don't keep in mind anything about last night. You were very silly." I replied, "So were you." I was somewhat cold with him, but still I thanked him for having me. I was glad I had bought them things while I was there.

Chapter Ten

Sri Lanka – Island of Serendipity

Thursday, 27th May 1976

Too long I have waited before writing in here once again. Several times, especially the other night, I had a strong desire to write, but then I was too tired, and too happy. I didn't want to waste precious moments. I am in Sri Lanka, an enchanted tropical island. I call it 'paradise island'. It is so beautiful here.

To continue with my story.... At Madras railway station I met an American called Len. We travelled to the ferry point together and took the ship across to Sri Lanka. The ship anchored close to the island, and we and some other passengers climbed into the small boat taking us to shore. When we landed, there were people waiting and as soon as I got off the boat I was asked if I had any saris to sell, so I straight away sold the sari I had brought for 140 Sri Lankan rupees (90 Indian rupees). In India I had paid 49 rupees so I was quite pleased.

We went for a walk along the beach which quickly became deserted after the boat had left. That night, Len and I camped on the veranda of a little half-ruined and deserted palm-thatched hut that we found there on the sand. It was idyllic. Next morning we took the train.

I fell in love with Sri Lanka immediately I stepped onto the island, so perfectly serene, exotic – it was a tropical paradise. Never have I seen such tall, slender, swaying palm trees, or so many in one place, or such lovely curving beaches as you might find on a lost island in the Pacific. I have seen such places only in films before. The people that live in that little town on the coast, with its small railway station and chugging steam train (two a day to the capital), live mostly in one or two roomed, palm-leaf thatched huts on the sea-shore or in the village and sell their giant pineapples for one Sri Lankan rupee each (or 10 paisa for a large slice) and their luscious coconuts for 25 paisa each. They also sell beautiful necklaces made of shells. There are tiny cafes with friendly owners selling pieces of sweet fudge made with jaggery, a very sweet juice which comes from the coconut tree. It is all so very clean compared with India.

We had been told that we would only be allowed to stay in Sri Lanka for one week because there is to be a Government Conference here this summer and tourists must leave during this time. We decided to travel to Colombo, the capital, to get a visa extension. It is the best capital city I have seen so far on my travels east. While in Colombo I went to a market and sold four lungies that I brought from India. If I had bought better quality lungies I could have made much more money, but still I was very pleased to sell them so easily and make a profit.

After Colombo we travelled to Kandy, also a pretty town, and the railway stations are so much cleaner and prettier than those in India. They look cared for.

In Kandy we visited a famous Buddhist temple called 'The Temple of the Tooth'. Supposedly the tooth of the Buddha is kept as a holy relic in a shrine inside the temple which is surrounded by a lake. In the evening we saw a religious procession from the temple – monks with shaven heads dressed in orange robes carrying baskets of burning coconuts on long poles; others were beating drums and were followed by two monks on the back of an elephant. It was quite a spectacle.

The Buddhist temples that I have seen here in Sri Lanka are quite beautiful and well-kept.

From Kandy we travelled by bus to Hikkaduwa, a beautiful village on the south west coast of Sri Lanka. We checked into a little guest house, and walked along the golden sands studded with wavering palm trees.

Here in Sri Lanka I feel that I have reached heaven. During my travels I have been wandering, unconsciously searching for a haven in which to rest – and here it is at last. I feel that I want to stay here on this island as long as possible, to rest, read, draw and write to my heart's content.

Len also wants to sightsee though, so in Hikkaduwa we went to see a rubber plantation and a tea factory.

We eat in little cafés. The food here is very spicy, like it is in South India. The Sri Lankans eat a lot of fish curry (far too spicy for me) with rice and grated coconut mixed together. Many of their curry sauces have a coconut milk base. The coconuts here are wonderful. Even the curd here is so much better than that in India – so thick and creamy. Perhaps the cows are in much better condition here and have more grass to eat.

I never intended to stay with Len so long – sometimes I just go along with things until the situation, or my better judgement, encourages me to leave. I like being with Len and having a travelling companion, but half of me would quite like to be alone again. I know that he is just hoping that I am going to let him sleep with me. I don't want to.

Friday, 28th May 1976

Len took the train this morning to Badulla. I decided not to go with him. I told him I would go later by bus.

I finally got fed up with him criticising me and telling me that all American girls have been on the pill since the age of seventeen. He tried to make me feel as though there was something wrong with me because I'm a virgin.

Actually I shall miss his company as a travelling companion, but only because I have got used to it. I have travelled with him longer than anybody else so far.

Saturday, 29th May 1976

I have arrived in Badulla and spent the night here in a lovely little guest house for five rupees a night. The owners went out of their way to find me a little room to myself as I was alone, and would not let me sleep in the dormitory where other travellers are sleeping. I would not have minded! They insisted on giving me one of their 'staff rooms'.

Bedulla is a delightful little town set in beautiful, hilly, green country. The scenery was spectacular on the way here and it was quite cold going through the mountains. I am longing to get to the coast again.

I thought I might see Len here in Bedulla but I have not. Possibly he has stopped at a town on the way as the train journey was very long. Maybe I shall see him when I go to Aragum Bay.

A Hut on the Beach
Tuesday, 1st June 1976

I am now in Aragum Bay. Again I have the feeling that I am in paradise. I have left the 'Rest House' (as the guest houses are so often called) that I was staying in here, and I am renting a hut made of thatched palm leaves, like the others in the village, on this beautiful beach for one rupee a day (five pence). This fishermen's hut village is beautiful and everything here looks clean.

I am so lucky because I have been given an especially nice hut with two small rooms – the front is a kind of veranda with an open doorway and two large windows (no glass of course) where I am now sitting. There is a wooden table and chair. Most of the rented huts I have seen do not have this table and chair.

This is just perfect for me as I want to do a lot of reading and writing – I want to write some children's stories. The back room of the hut is my bedroom. There is a camp bed in it – made of wood and soft rough fabric material – and there are two shelves which are created with planks of wood suspended by rope from the ceiling! There is one little window at the back of the hut with wooden sticks tied to it like bars and a thatched door with a chain and a padlock to this room leading from the veranda. However, I have taken the precaution of burying my passport and money in the sand floor. The sand is beautifully soft and fine. I also have two woven mats in the hut which is a luxury too.

The local people and their families who live in the huts round about are so friendly. Just now, several of them came up to chat with me in broken English and asked if I would like a pot of curd (2 rupees 50 paisa for a big pot) and honey which one lady here has offered me free as a present.

There are quite a few young travellers staying in huts around about me – so far I have spoken to Australians and Americans – and all are very friendly. Australians are here for the surf – there are strong waves here and you can rent a surf board for one rupee a day from the hut owner. In the curved bay there is also a beautifully calm spot of clear blue sea for bathing, just across the sand from my hut.

These friendly villagers have just come to chat again – boys, girls and women, along with the hut owner. He is a very friendly person. I have just ordered a bottle of liquid jaggery (which they call coconut honey) for six rupees and a pot of curd to eat every day. I shall eat and drink the coconuts and pineapples here too and have a meal of curry and rice cooked by the local women who live with their families in the huts next to mine. A meal only costs three rupees a day, but sometimes I shall go into town to eat. One of the women just brought me a plate of fried potatoes topped with the yolk of an egg, as a gift.

I love the way the women dress here in colourful lungies wrapped around their bodies (like my wrap-around skirt) and sari tops (blouses) showing their midriffs. They do not wear saris. Their clothes are so simple and suited to the climate. I am wearing something similar.

Now I am writing this diary and eating curd by candlelight. I feel very contented.

Len and another American guy are staying in a hut nearby. They arrived here yesterday. My emotions are so crazy – I miss him. I was feeling quite lonely until these villagers came and chatted to me. I don't know whether Len feels that I rejected him by not sleeping with him or whether he has now rejected me, but it was me who decided to take the bus instead of the train. Len is sharing a hut with another American man. I suppose he met him on the train.

I don't actually mind being alone. Rarely on the whole of my travels have I ever felt lonely or afraid for more than a few minutes. Life is so simple here, and people are so friendly.

Now it is so dark. I can see I shall be going to bed early in this place. I'll go over to the little tea shop (another hut) and see the other travellers here now.

Wednesday, 2nd June 1976

I'm not even sure if this is the right date.

Here I am still in this paradise sitting in my little house. The whole village must be asleep except me. It should be about eleven o'clock now, though time means nothing here. People tell time by the position of the sun in the sky. At sunset they eat and get ready for bed because the nights are so pitch black. They rise at dawn – about five o'clock – and the sunrises are so beautiful, but at first it is hard to get used to these timings.

I want to stay here longer on this beautiful beach. I love being so close to nature. I am not so keen on the nights though. Every now and again an enormous bug comes into the hut under the door or through the window. If I was asleep, I wouldn't see them. Mostly the insects don't worry me but they do at night. I even started to worry about wild animals last night. Behind the beach there is a jungle-like area. I have seen wild monkeys running about there and climbing in the trees when I walked along the country road to the town yesterday. I think there are crocodiles in the river here. I have also seen elephants on this island, especially working elephants, but I am not afraid of them. There is so much wild life in Sri Lanka. It is like an open safari park.

Yesterday I stayed too long in the town and missed the six o'clock evening bus back, and then it was too dark to walk the mile and a half back home to our hut village on the beach. I didn't want to wait until ten o'clock for the next bus. One of the local village boys was in town with his bike. He gave me a ride on his cross-bar back to the village and refused to take any payment for it. How nice the local people are. I have nearly always found them to be so to me. Some people seem to have more trouble with them and I think it is because of their own attitude, their own mistrust – perhaps some travellers expect the worse and that's what they get. However, perhaps I am lucky.

Sunday, 6th June 1976

Len left early on Thursday morning with his friend. I woke up just a few minutes before they came out of their hut to go. I saw the torch light. I think I picked up their vibrations.

After Len had gone, I started to miss him again, but now I have gradually regained my feeling of contentment and tranquillity in this lovely place. I have met so many other good-looking men here with nice personalities. They are nearly all Australians. There are three brothers travelling together – one with his wife and another with his girlfriend. The other brother saw me and invited me to have lunch with them – curd and fruit and treacle which they mix up themselves. Bruce also suggested that in the mornings I go up to the 'point' of the bay where they all surf.

There is a small hut tea-shop there, selling tea made with tinned condensed milk, coconut cakes and bananas. The tea-shop is really a thatched palm parasol supported by sticks, with a wooden table under it. It is set in a little sandy grove up in the dunes surrounded by palm trees, bushes and undergrowth. There everyone sits around and chats and drinks tea in between surfing. There are a few new people here now – but very few women – four of us now in the whole company, I think, and I am the only free single one!

One of the Sri Lankan boys who live in the beach village here runs the tea-shop. He is thirteen years old and everyone is very fond of him. His name is Pali. Another small boy helps him. They open their tea-shop at the break of dawn when the surfers go up to the 'point', and in the evening they serve tea to us at a little table in a different, similar tea-shop – another thatched parasol in the hut area where Pali and the Australians live. There are several compounds of huts and each compound has a palm fence around it. There are quite a few monkeys around and some beautiful, brightly coloured birds which I have seen amongst the palm trees on the beach. We also saw a scorpion the other night and some people saw a snake up a tree at the 'point'.

Quite a few stray dogs are also running around. They wander about eating whatever they can find, which mostly consists of any scraps thrown to them – not many. The dogs are scraggy and thin. The locals sometimes treat them cruelly and often hit them with sticks if they come too near or try to steal food. The dogs, however, are so gentle, it is unbelievable.

Doug's wife, a Japanese girl, feeds the dogs in her area and so I decided to feed the black puppy that is in my compound. It is a dear little thing, so gentle and loving. There are two more dogs in this area. I gave two of them something to eat today and they both waited patiently while I fed the other and watched me so trustingly.

I can't believe that dogs which are often treated so brutally should be so gentle, but they are. I think that not all stray dogs would be, though, and I am still sometimes afraid of dogs that I don't know, but I know these dogs well enough now to know that they are not aggressive.

The dogs came to see me tonight and I fed them again. They rush up to me, licking my hands and wagging their tails, but when I go into my hut they don't venture in. Probably too many times they have been turned out of huts. I wish I could take that puppy home. It has got such lovely, endearing dark eyes.

More Island Adventures
Tuesday, 15th June 1976

I have now left the paradise of Aragum Bay, after staying eleven days. I left on the 5.30 bus on the 12th June. If the bus had not come that morning I would not have gone. Never have I felt so sorry to leave a place – I thought I was going to cry. I did not realise how fond I had grown of that black puppy either, but I did know, every minute that I was there, how much I appreciated living in that little fishermen's village on the beach. I felt so rich there – richer than I have ever felt in my life. There I had my own little house in that idyllic place with all facilities that I needed and all comforts, although actually I had nothing.

What I loved most, was that I could live so simply and so close to the earth; I could live life in all its fullness and yet I had so few needs. I lacked nothing. I used to wake up in the morning and rejoice that there was another day to live. I wanted to wake up early so as not to waste any of those precious hours of daylight. The morning sunrise was especially beautiful – the sun's rays shed a kind of translucent light over everything, which is special only to those early hours.

I sometimes used to ask my neighbours to wake me up at sunrise or just before when they went out surfing, and then after a few moments of lying peacefully on my bed I would get up and slip on my bikini and fetch my towel. If it was early enough, I would go over to Raja's hut where his wife, Barby, cooked hoppers in a metal pot over an open fire on the sand floor. They cost 25 paisa each, and an egg hopper cost 75 paisa. (There are a hundred paisa in each rupee.)

Hoppers are made of brown rice flour and have a soft bread-like consistency. Barby would spoon the batter mixture into the pan – making thick rounds, and when they were nearly cooked she poured a little coconut milk on the top or broke an egg onto it. These hoppers were always served at about six o'clock in the morning. If I got up too late I would go straight down to the sea to swim, sometimes stopping at Raja's tea-shop for tea made with condensed milk, or a 'drinking coconut' with a straw. At other times I would swim first in that beautiful clear blue sea – it always felt wonderful to swim on an empty stomach. I took delight in feeling fit and trimming up my body as I swam so much and I did not think much about food.

After swimming, I would wander up to Pali's little tea-shop amongst the palms at the back of the beach, then I would go back and swim in the sea again until lunch-time when I would go back to Raja's hut and eat salad, or curd and fruit, or coconut hoppers. They were delicious but I never had more than two at a time. I used to rest around midday when it was hottest and the sun was high in the sky, because I had got sunburnt when I first arrived. In the afternoon I went visiting for a short while, and once I attended the 'Bong Session' – a whole group of the Australian men would sit and smoke marijuana for a few hours and get stoned every afternoon! I didn't share in the marijuana – but I sat with them.

The water was not too salty or sandy, but after swimming I went to the village well and drew out cool water to pour all over my body. The bucket was extended on a rope from a large wooden stick and swung from its support like a see-saw. Drawing up water is so easy and effortless – it is a marvellous invention. I would always go swimming again in the afternoon – the afternoons are beautifully breezy.

Sometimes I would go walking before sunset along that lovely desolate beach or along the little winding road into the town. It was quite a long but beautiful walk. Once I sat down by the bank of a small, still lake on which there were primitive wooden boats – probably for fishing – and I watched the sunset. The sunsets are as beautiful as the sunrises.

One day I was there looking at the beautiful coloured birds in the trees and a lot of monkeys playing, when suddenly someone called out my name – it was an American guy that I had met on the bus on the way to the Rest House. He had been travelling with his brother and his brother's girlfriend and had left with them, but now he had come back. He is a very nice person. I think he liked me, but I did not want to have any kind of relationship with him. When I left Aragum Bay things were getting a bit awkward because both he and my Australian hut neighbour were getting a bit friendly with me and I would have had to choose one or reject both in the end!

I went for a moonlit walk with my Australian neighbour one night. His name was Bruce and I was very physically attracted to him, but he was too extrovert a personality for me.

Every night after sunset, we all went to the tea-shop for a couple of hours till about eight o'clock, after which we went back to our huts to sleep. On the night of the full moon just before I left, we had a party on the beach.

I love living without electricity. I only had to light a couple of small candles at night for a few minutes while I found my toothbrush and laid out my sleeping bag on the camp bed.

Sometimes at sunset I would eat the meal of fish and rice for three rupees that Raja's mother cooked. I felt that it was good to buy their food as the village people do not make much profit and this is a way to help them, but I was giving half the meal to my stray dogs. That little puppy used to dance after me when I took the plate of food into my own hut.

One evening Raja's mother saw me feeding it and she did not look happy. The locals used to laugh at me when I fondled the dogs. They could not understand us westerners for our treatment of the dogs. I suppose they are so poor that they cannot afford to have pets – they need to feed their families – and mostly they and their children all sleep in the same one or two roomed huts. They rely on the money the men make from fishing. The surroundings here are much more idyllic than those of the beach hut villages in India though.

Wednesday, 16th June 1976

I wish now that I had stayed longer in Aragum Bay. Here I am stuck at Talamainar Pier, where I can't even swim, for they tell me there are dangerous shell fish in the water with sharp spikes, and anyway, it is dirty. I have to wait until Friday morning for the ferry. I am finally going back across to India.

I have had some adventures since I left Aragum Bay – now at least I have time to write in this diary and catch up with my news.

Today I was entertained at lunch time by the customs officers I met at the station. They gave me a huge lunch of rice and crab curry. I don't like eating crab actually as I can picture them alive on the beach and I am not sure whether they boil them while they are still alive. I have decided I am never going to eat crab again. Also, my body has become so fit with all the swimming that I don't want to eat big meals that make me feel bloated like the one they gave me. These customs men are coming to visit me again at the Rest House this evening. I suppose it will pass the time – I am the only one staying there.

After leaving Aragum Bay I had a long, hot journey with

three changes of buses. It takes a ridiculously long time to travel only a few miles.

At about three o'clock in the afternoon, I was waiting for the next bus which probably never came. Suddenly a car stopped at a nearby cafe. Three German men were travelling in a chauffer-driven car. They gave me a lift to Trimcomalee. The biggest, fattest one squeezed in the front with me and pushed his arm around my shoulders so that I sweated throughout the whole trip – although less than I would have done on the bus, I am sure, and I was grateful for the ride. They invited me to travel around the island with them for the next three days sharing petrol costs but I decided against it. It was too expensive anyway.

I stayed in Trimcomalee for two nights. It was a lovely little town but not half as nice as Aragum Bay though the water was beautiful for swimming – so calm and clear. I had a room to myself in a guest house. On the first night the hotel boy (who looked about twenty years old) kept knocking on my door.

Thursday, 17th June 1976

My diary writing yesterday was interrupted by some Naval Officers who came to talk to me while I was sitting writing on the beach, looking longingly at the sea. They told me that bathing was safe after all, so I stripped off (I had my bikini underneath) and went in swimming with them for half an hour. It was lovely – I tried to forget about the spiky shellfish! But anyway, I never saw any until I came out of the water and then I did see one empty large shell with sharp spikes lying on the sand. It is beautiful and I have kept it as a souvenir. We swam until sunset and then I went back to my guest house. They treated me respectfully.

I must finish writing about my experience in Trimcomalee. The hotel boy kept knocking on my door and eventually I opened it to tell him to leave me in peace. He had brought me some bread and jam, of all things! I then realised I was famished, as I have been practically starving myself in order to get fitter and fitter, living on curd and fruits and a few nuts – although I also ate eggs and 'hoppers' occasionally. I accepted the bread and jam with thanks which was a foolish thing to do, because after a few minutes he was at the door again with 'string hoppers' but this time I did not open it, telling him through the door that I was tired and wanted to sleep.

The next day he was a bit of a nuisance and hurt his foot when I was pushing the door closed on him. He pretended to be angry at that and said, "I will stick a knife in your stomach." He said, "Maybe tonight."

I suspected that he was trying to frighten me. I ignored it, but that night I inspected the doors in my room and discovered that one of them (two doors together) pushed open quite easily into the dormitory room next door where no one was sleeping. This gave me quite a shock. I then put the bolt down and felt safer though I suspected that the bolt was not very secure. I was quite right – it wasn't!

In the middle of the night I awoke suddenly feeling the presence of someone leaning over me and a hand was shoved over my mouth. I knew immediately who it was. I let out a piercing scream and then shouted at him to get out of my room hoping that someone might come to my aid. (I knew there were other travellers in the hotel.) The boy tore out of my room afraid that he would be discovered. I groped about the room looking for the candle. I had no light because they had given me a fan – by request – and it was plugged into the light bulb! I grabbed my skirt and put it on, giving up the idea of finding the candle.

I went along the corridor to the next room where I knew there was a young American traveller sleeping. I had shared my curd with him at midday in exchange for some of his pineapple. I knocked on his door and then discovered that his door was locked from the outside. There was a large key in the lock! It was obvious that the hotel boy had locked him in! I unlocked the door and called out. My friend opened the door and I explained what had happened and asked if I could sleep in his room – I knew there was another bed in the room. He agreed at once and I went back to fetch all my things. He came to help me.

I was curious as to how the hotel boy had entered my room but after inspecting those two doors again I discovered that the one I had not bolted, opened from the outside. The bolt was on the outside and it swung open easily. The boy had known about the door obviously, and had planned this! I was just collecting my bags and my friend was helping me when the hotel boy appeared again and for a second switched off the hall light which I had switched on! Then he noticed, when I said in a loud voice, "I am not staying in here tonight", that someone else was with me. He turned on the light quickly and played innocent saying, "What happened?"

I replied, "You know perfectly well what happened. I'm moving my things next door. I will tell the manager."

Next morning the American guy had to leave early, but before he left, the hotel boy came into our room and convincingly acting so innocent – offering to go to the market to buy the cloves for me that I had enquired about the day before – that my American friend said, "I really don't think he knew what was going on – he was trying to be helpful."

I told the boy that I could get the cloves myself! He whispered to me, "Don't tell anyone."

Later when my American friend had gone, I asked the boy why he did it. He didn't have any answer to give. He merely looked at me timidly and asked whether I had told the American. I said, "Yes, of course" and that I might tell others too. I said to him, "I won't come back here again."

Afterwards I went out to the market to get some curd and fruit for my breakfast – I did not feel guilty about bringing it in from outside – and then I went swimming. When I got back, the hotel boy brought me some coconut milk, and wrote down the names of shops in which I could buy cloves.

When I left in the afternoon, he shook hands with me and smiled timidly, wishing me a safe journey.

I realise now that I should have reported him to the manager for the sake of others, but I didn't. I don't know why I didn't. I just said to him, "What you did to me, don't ever do to anyone else."

After I had left the hotel I realised how much it had shaken me up. I always check all the doors at night now, although last night in this hotel where I feel safe, I did open the door in the night because I felt so hot and longed for some air. It led out into the garden.

I stayed one night in Anuradhapura and then I went to Polonnaruwa and hired a bicycle for a couple of hours so that I could ride out and see some historical ruins. I saw a gigantic statue of the Buddha lying on his side surrounded by trees – the Gal Vihara statue. It is fourteen metres long and was made in 1200 AD. It is a wonderful statue. When I got there, I met some American girls that I had seen in Aragum Bay chatting to Len and his friend. I felt a bit awkward with them because

I had felt jealous at the time. It was silly of me but I did not want to take the train with them that night to Talaimanar so I stayed and took the bus next day. Now I am glad because I would have arrived here even earlier!

Chapter Eleven

A Boat Ride through Kerala and on to Goa

Saturday, 19th June 1976

I am now back in south India on a bumpy train journey from Madurai to Quilon on the south-west coast. I don't think I'll be writing much tonight unless the train starts travelling more smoothly!

The boat trip across from Sri Lanka to India was delightful – I love boat trips. However, I felt sad to leave my beautiful island. The customs officers who had bought me lunch before also ordered lunch for me on the boat – a big curry – and there was also curd and chocolate for dessert. There was so much that I could not eat anything else for the rest of the day. I thought to myself how ironical it was – I had been scared of going through Customs because I lied about my money situation when I entered Sri Lanka. Perhaps they would not have let me in if I had told them that I only had two hundred dollars. I bought my boat ticket with cash and I wrote on the form they gave me, that I had five hundred dollars in travellers' cheques. I was afraid that they would ask to see them, but luckily they did not. Now I have brought some cloves from Sri Lanka to sell in India. I have brought the legal amount (one kilo) plus one extra pound which is a risk, so I was cheating the Customs all round. Then I was met by the very officers I was fearing and I was entertained by them!

Going through the Customs when I arrived back in India was more of a hassle. They inspected my carrier bag of books in which I also had my extra pound parcel of cloves! The other kilo was inside my rucksack. I think if they had found that I had brought more than the legal limit, they would have confiscated them or perhaps made me pay a fine. I can't afford to lose forty rupees. If I can sell them, I should be able to make a good profit, especially further north, but I must not tempt fate by getting too greedy.

How I appreciate Sri Lanka now I am back in India again. It did me so much good. That heavenly island was one of my dreams come true. When I was there I experienced an inner tranquillity, a stillness, and I no longer desired to keep travelling. It was as though I had found what I had unconsciously been searching for, and all I then had to do was stay in one place and drink in that wonderful joy. My soul came to rest. Now I wait for a future date when I can return and stay longer. I feel happy just to know that that place exists.

I have written a song about the island:

Song of the Island of Serendipity:

I searched every temple,
the teachings, the creeds,
to conquer my thirst
and to answer my need.
But island of beauty and island of love
in you I have found what I sought from above.

Not in the temples of Hindu and Jain.
Not in the churches, again and again.
But there on that island
my spirit found rest.
The treasures of Heaven
there answered my quest.

Sunday, 20th June 1976

5.30 a.m.

It is still dark. The sun has not yet risen. I arrived at Quilon about an hour ago – 4.30 a.m. I read in my guide book that there is a boat going up the coast to Cochin at 5 o'clock but they tell me here that there is not one until 10 o'clock so I must wait in this cafe by the waterside. I have already eaten a large breakfast for the sake of something to do.

When I arrived at Rameswarum, the first town in India, I spent the evening with an American couple there. We looked around the interesting town and incredible tiered temple with its bazaar inside. There I bought some cheap handicrafts and a set of woven palm-leaf baskets – there are five of them – each of which fits inside the others so that the very smallest one is inside them all, like a Russian doll. This set of baskets only costs two rupees! Such a lot of work for the craftsman for so little money! I gave him three rupees which also isn't much.

Interesting as Rameswarum was, I felt a bit depressed after leaving lovely Sri Lanka. India feels strange and foreign now I have come back to it, whereas Sri Lanka never did. I am again conscious of the very many people crowding the streets here. Sri Lankan towns are never overcrowded like this. In Indian towns there are so many people that I start to feel that the human race is like a swarm of insects crawling on the Earth everywhere destroying the planet – there are too many humans and this seems to reduce the feeling of the value of individual human life.

I have seen such horrific sights in India – poor people living in makeshift shacks with roofs of filthy rags, women washing their clothes in dirty half-dried-up pools of water, deformed beggars, starving dogs – the list goes on and on. I have been so shocked that I can never forget what I have seen.

In Sri Lanka where the population is much less, I did not see even poor people living in such awful conditions. Life seems to be a wonderful treasure on that island. Nature is unspoilt. There is room also for wild animals. Not so in India, where human beings are everywhere and poverty is so evident. It shocks me that human beings live in unthinkable conditions after all these thousands (or millions) of years of being on the Earth. You never see birds living in poverty or overcrowded conditions, nor have I ever seen wild monkeys living in such a way – all the monkeys I have seen in India look well-fed and healthy. They do not live in poverty!

One thing Sri Lanka seems to lack, however, is handicrafts. They have shell necklaces, and painted masks used in devil dancing (to scare off evil spirits) for sale, but not much else. On the contrary, India is rich in handicrafts. Labour is so cheap here and there is so much competition for jobs.

I took the train with my American friends to Madurai. That is also an interesting town with another incredible temple – there are some wonderful temples in south India. Meenakshi Temple in Madurai is enormous, with thousands of figures of gods carved on the outside of the building. Inside there is an enormous tank of water, a bazaar and a temple museum, as well as the usual inner sanctuaries where unfortunately non-Hindus are not allowed to go. Strings of scented jasmine flowers and sweets are sold as usual on stalls in the temple courtyards for the pilgrims to buy as offerings to the gods.

The market stalls and shops in Madurai town are very interesting. I spent all morning and half of the afternoon walking around the streets and then went back and rested in the hotel room which I had booked, thinking I would stay there the night.

When I discovered that there was a night train to Quilon, I was annoyed that I had taken the room, and I tried to get my money back, but the hotel owner would not give it to me. I had an argument with him. People stood and watched, but anyway, I am used to them watching everything I do! However, complain as I did, it did no good – I still had to pay for the room. Afterwards, however, I was glad that I had it, for I was so tired and hot by 2.30 p.m. that I was glad to go back and take a shower and sleep. I caught the train at 7.40 p.m. and had a very pleasant journey. In my carriage where I had a reserved seat, there were few people and I could lie down.

9.30 a.m.

I am now sitting on the ferry boat. We have to wait another half an hour before it starts.

This morning I left my luggage in the cafe and took a rickshaw to the beach where I walked for two hours. I was

A Boat Ride through Kerala and on to Goa

hoping I could swim, but I attracted too much attention merely by walking along the beach, which even at that early hour, was quite filled with men, women and children from the fishing huts all along the sand. Many of them were doing their morning toilet in the sand! Everyone stared at me, but I am used to that. Some called out to me but I didn't speak to anybody until the very last moments, when I was just leaving the beach. I communicated by sign language to a group of women and then drank a cup of chai in a little teashop. The people there seemed pleased. There were no westerners anywhere in sight at all.

These huts on the beach are similar to those in Sri Lanka, but there are so many of them here crowded together in dirty conditions on this long beach. There is rubbish strewn about everywhere. The scene is not as picturesque as it is in Sri Lanka; there is a totally different atmosphere in these Indian fishing villages. In Sri Lanka the beaches are so deserted with just a remote fishing village here and there. It is said that everybody can have a beach to himself in Sri Lanka. That could not be said of India. However, Quilon is a pleasant little town with rivers lined with dense palm trees and a few saw mills. I saw many logs waiting to go up the river. I also saw an elephant transporting logs. There are quite a few little shops here. I walked all the way back from the beach to the river ferry as I had so much time.

Now the boat is moving. It is going to be a beautiful trip along this waterway – so many palm trees and wooden canoe-like boats all along the banks, and a pleasant breeze is blowing.

Friday, 25th June 1976

That trip through the winding waterways was beautiful, but after ten hours of it I was quite pleased to get off the boat, and

I was exhausted. I slept at the bus station that night in one of their Rest Rooms – five rupees a night – quite cheap and very clean. Next day I got up late after a good rest, caught the train from Cochin to Bangalore, spending a night on the train, and then spent the day in Bangalore before continuing my journey to Goa.

In Bangalore I was searching for the Spiritual Museum which is mentioned in my guide book. I went to enquire about it in a college in the town. One of the students offered to take me there on his motor scooter. After that he spent the whole day with me which was pleasant because I did have another ten hours to wait for my train which was not leaving until 8 o'clock in the evening.

We were shown around the Spiritual Museum by the 'Sisters' who are in charge of the place. I think they live there. They all wear white saris and live like nuns but say they don't belong to any religious order. One of them who could speak good English explained everything to me. She said they aim to live a pure life and practise Raja Yoga, a form of meditation, which they say gives them peace of mind and spirit and will ultimately lead them to the Divine.

They believe that the world goes through cycles, passing through a new age every few thousand years. The first age was the golden age of the gods when the world was a utopia. They believe in the karma of the soul – and that the poorest people are now suffering for their misdeeds of their past lives. I suppose it is a way to explain away the poverty. This idea I dislike but some of their other ideas are quite beautiful. I like their central philosophy of meditation and I like the fact that they are vegetarians.

The student who had come with me there took me for lunch in a little restaurant – rice plate – the main south Indian dish. I have had it before in south India. It consists of a plate of several small bowls containing different things: rice, buttermilk, curd, spicy dal, (thin lentil soup), and a thin vegetable curry, usually. All this costs only one rupee per plate which is very cheap and has some nutritional value. It's nice to have these traditional dishes occasionally and I enjoyed it very much.

Afterwards my friend took me to his home to meet his family. They were lovely people. He has no mother, but he, his father, his brothers and their wives, and one sister, all live together in a large house which he showed me around. He told me that a marriage had been arranged for his eighteen-year-old sister four days previously to a boy who is distantly related. She is to be married in August and until that day she will see her future husband only about once a week or every ten days, but they will not go out together. He told me that his father will also arrange his own marriage in a couple of years.

I am so glad that I don't live here! How I appreciate being free to meet many different people. When I first started travelling and I was feeling so confused about my relationships with the opposite sex, I almost envied the Indian women – everything seems so simple and easy for them – they would not be criticised for being virgins before marriage, or for not wanting to have sex. I have almost felt persecuted by both cultures: Indians have disapproved of me for what they thought I was – a permissive, liberated, amoral woman travelling around alone; and American men wrote me off, so it felt, as a psychologically hung-up, immature individual who had not experimented with sex by the age of twenty-two, unlike American girls.

Both cultures, though, seem to deny me the right of freedom to be myself – to choose for myself what I do and how I conduct myself. Freedom to be oneself must surely be the most fundamental right of every living being.

However, I think that sex, when both partners are in agreement and in love, is surely a beautiful and sacred act, not an ugly thing to be despised and hushed up as it seems to be portrayed in eastern society. Nature has created it for us, after all.

Goa in the Monsoon
Saturday, 26th June 1976

I am in Goa. I have been here for a few days and now I want to catch up with the news again!

I was fortunate enough to meet up with a Canadian traveller on the way here. He was sitting in the railway restaurant waiting for the train – we had to change trains. We sat together and chatted throughout the journey and I have grown to like him during our few days together. He is a very sweet person.

A Boat Ride through Kerala and on to Goa

His name is Daniel and he has a very unassuming, gentle nature. He makes me feel peaceful and calm, unlike Len who I travelled with in Sri Lanka who argued and criticised me all the time.

I arrived in Goa with Daniel and we found a hotel together in Panjib, the capital. Goa is a delightful state – so unlike the rest of India that we felt as though we had entered a different country. It seems much cleaner and there is less poverty and overcrowding.

I could not believe it when I saw Indian women getting on the train with short, permed hairdos, high-heeled shoes, mini-skirts and even make-up – dressed like westerners. Actually they wear the kinds of clothes that we wore in the sixties in England ten years ago. What a contrast they are to the conventional Indian women in other states, with their beautiful saris and their long waist-length hair tied back, and their clear skins. In fact, I prefer the way the women dress everywhere else in India. I don't really like this imitation of the west in Goa. The women in traditional dress look far more beautiful. Who cares for western fashions! I like the anklets that many Indian women wear around their ankles. I think fashion is really just a matter of what you get used to seeing.

Many people in Goa are Roman Catholics because it was a Portuguese colony for so long – up until only a decade ago. I have read that the people in this state were forced through violent means to convert to Christianity and change their lifestyle and give up their Indian culture.

Goa reminds me of Europe – we could be in Spain or Portugal. Some of the little towns here are prettier than those I have seen in the rest of India.

There are souvenir shops like those you find in sea-side towns in Europe, and the countryside is quite beautiful with many palm trees, winding roads, rivers and lakes. There are houses dotted here and there in little groves of palm trees, and villages tucked away amid forests and hills. The beaches are lovely too, and I can imagine that in the tourist season it is like paradise here when the sea is turquoise blue and calm, and the sunrises and sunsets are as magnificent as they are in Sri Lanka. Certainly it does remind me a little of Sri Lanka except that I saw more wild life, especially elephants in Sri Lanka, and also I think the Buddhist religion creates a lovelier atmosphere on the island. The island of Sri Lanka seems more relaxed, more laid back. Goa seems to be trying to be too western.

Goa is not as overcrowded as the rest of India, or as poverty stricken. Perhaps the Portuguese did more for their colony than the British did for the rest of India. I have read that the British cut down most of the forests in India and left vast, dry plains to be scorched by the sun so that nothing would grow there anymore.

When trees are there, they provide shade that keeps water in the ground and this nourishes the soil and vegetation and the wild-life that live in it. Trees provide oxygen as well as fruit and herbs and medicinal plants for the villagers that live there.

The British used elephants in this work of cutting down the forests – elephants whose home had been the forest, so when the forests were gone they had nowhere to go. Why did the British do this? Obviously they did not understand the importance of life-sustaining forests.

In Goa there is still so much forest and it makes the scenery beautiful and keeps the air much purer. There is less dust and pollution and the environment is much more pleasant, and much more green, even though the climate is just as hot as it is on the dried-up, bare, yellow plains of India that I saw through the windows of the trains, especially in the north.

I think that a few hundred years ago, the whole of India, covered in forest, was perhaps like Goa and Sri Lanka, with scattered villages and pure water streams and rivers. The west has brought so much pollution to India in the way of industry, and destroyed the land by cutting down the trees. It makes me feel so sad.

I have been reading a book about the Freedom Movement in India. The atrocities done by the British here during their rule are quite horrifying. I was disgusted to read how the British behaved.

India has been a conquered nation for so long — for hundreds of years. It used to be one of the most civilised nations on the Earth — one of the most advanced and wealthiest cultures — but for hundreds of years other nations have come to conquer it and plunder its wealth, and they drained many of its natural resources, as well as its gold and jewels.

It was not for nothing that the British Empire called India, 'the jewel in its crown'. In the time of the British, the cotton grown in India was transported to England and made into cloth there. Indians were not allowed to make cloth and the people in that trade sometimes starved to death.

The manufacture of salt was forbidden in India — Mahatma Ghandi led a famous march to the sea to collect salt. Meetings of more than a few people in one place were also forbidden in case there was a rebellion against British rule. In 1919, in Amritsar, Northern India, peaceful crowds including women and children gathered to hear a speaker belonging to the Freedom Movement, and were all massacred on the orders of a British General called Dyer.

Before that, in 1857, there was an Indian Mutiny against the rule of the British East India Company and the British took terrible revenge. There is a statue in London honouring the man who crushed the Mutiny. I think that statue should be pulled down!

India believes in non-violence, so for a long time they did not fight back and there were not many rebellions. However, I feel that the philosophy of non-violence in India is a supreme example to the world. It is wonderful how friendly the Indians are to foreigners travelling in their land.

I have come to the conclusion that Britain only became a great power because of its exploitation of other nations, otherwise how could such a small country ever have become so rich and powerful as it did in Victorian times? Even so, the money remained only with the rich minority. Most of the population in Britain remained poor. It was not the fault of the ordinary British people – they cannot be blamed for it – but of their rulers.

Reading the truth about the British Empire that we never read in our own history books makes me feel very ashamed. These books that tell the truth about what happened in the past in India were banned while the British were here, and their authors were imprisoned just as Mahatma Ghandi was imprisoned so many times. His wife died in jail.

Now I want to write more about Goa!

Daniel and I stayed in a little hotel in Panjib. We shared a room because it was cheaper than having a room each. My relationship with him has been platonic as usual, but it was nice not to be grabbed as soon as I lay down on the bed as I have been by some other men! As I have got to know him, I have developed a strong liking for him. He is a lovely man.

Daniel has only just started his tour of India and can afford to sightsee and splurge his money whereas I have to be careful with my money. I will be returning to England to go back to college in September. Daniel has come across from Australia and south-east Asia.

What a surprise – in Panjib there are little bars stocked with liquor, and western music! We had a very pleasant evening sitting in the one attached to our hotel and we drank bottled beer. I did enjoy the western music. There were several groups of Indian men and boys sitting in the bar, but only one girl came in with someone, probably her husband. I feel sorry for the youth of this country but I think that they are perhaps a little more modern in Goa, though I expect the parents are still very strict.

I have drained Daniel of knowledge about Thailand, Indonesia and Malaysia and learned about the beautiful beaches there. How I love beaches. He tells me that there are also some wonderful beaches in Australia.

Today, after walking around the town, Daniel and I took the bus and ferry to Calangute beach, which I hear is full of westerners in the high season: winter. We travelled through some lovely countryside and arrived at the village on the beach.

We have put up in a hotel called 'Tourist Hotel'. It costs ten rupees between us for this lovely room – very clean – with attached bathroom and two beds. The hotel is right on the beach and opposite are a few little restaurants and restaurant bars where we eat Indian and western foods. There are delicious milk-shakes also. You always find milk-shakes in the places where young people stay in Goa.

There are few westerners around as this is the low season, though we have seen a few who are renting houses among the palm trees behind the beach. We were offered a house for a week for thirty-five rupees, but we do not want to stay a week. In the tourist season it would cost about twenty rupees a night for a house, but usually many young people share one house.

Although I have been to some less pleasant places in India, still I feel happy that I have seen much more of India than many other travellers have – and I have seen the real

India, not just a Portuguese colony that is more like Europe than India.

I wanted to go swimming, and in fact I have, but the sea is rough because now the rainy season, the monsoon, is approaching fast. It did rain yesterday and today for a couple of hours in the afternoon but the rest of the day has been sunny – not too hot, but pleasant. Certainly the temperature here in this rainy season is better than the heat I experienced in the dried-up northern plains of India. Daniel and I went for a walk along the palm-studded beach today and it began to pour with rain – we got drenched. When it rains here in the monsoon, it really does rain!

This evening we sat again in one of the little restaurant bars listening to western music and drinking coffee. Here the other few westerners congregate at the little tables and we chatted with an English girl and her German friend. Perhaps she was in her late twenties. She said she had come to India to do research on Indian dance and is writing a book. Two years ago she lived in Delhi and started a drama group which she is going back to visit. She was very well-spoken and said she had attended a boarding school in India.

All the young people I have met travelling have been very well-educated, usually university students, and many come from wealthy families. Australians especially travel a lot. Travelling around as I am doing is still quite uncommon in England, and I have never had much money and I don't come from a rich family. I am just spending what I have saved in the last few months. I was inspired by my elder brother, Tony, who loves travelling the world.

I think most people in the west are so afraid of losing their securities that they are unable to take off spontaneously and travel to unknown places. People spend their lives 'building' and gathering possessions as soon as they can because this makes them feel safe. It is so much more exciting to live in this

A Boat Ride through Kerala and on to Goa

supreme insecurity, to see life in all its colours, to see how the poor people live, and to live like them for a few days also. I think travelling the world is the best education anybody can have.

I have always felt that there are things much more valuable than money in this life. I feel rich without having much money – I feel as though the whole world belongs to me to roam in. I always remember that saying of Jesus: "Blessed are the meek for they shall inherit the Earth." I think 'meek' means 'non-aggressive', and inheriting the Earth means to wander in it anywhere I want to go.

Sunday, 27th June 1976

I have left Goa now and I am on the train again. While I was waiting for the train at the station I was talking to someone, an old man, who was also waiting for a train. He said to me, "You are such a small, small girl travelling all alone." It made me laugh.

I have also just had a long conversation with a university professor who was sitting in my carriage on this train. People everywhere are so friendly. He asked me about my life and travels and finally I told him that last year I was a teacher in a primary school for a year but I gave up my job to come travelling. Then, before he got off the train, he turned to me and said, "I have to make an apology to you. When I first met you I thought you were a hippy."

This also made me laugh, although I have been told this a hundred times! I wonder what a hippy really is! I still don't know the difference between travellers and hippies! They think we are all hippies!

I told him I am on my way up the west coast of India where I hope to meet the Magic Bus in Delhi which will take me back to England, but I possibly might stop in Pune★ to visit an ashram. I got out my notebook where I have written the name and address of the place that was mentioned at the back of the book I saw in Amsterdam called, *My Way, The Way of the White Clouds* and showed it to him.

I was so surprised because he immediately recognised the name of the spiritual Master, Osho★, who gave the discourses recorded in that book. He said, "Yes, you must go and see this man. I have a lot of love and respect for him." He told me he had been a fellow professor at the same university as him, years ago. What a coincidence!

I wonder whether I have the energy to visit any more places. I had decided that if the train stops in Pune I will get off but if it doesn't then I won't. However, I have been told that the train is going to stop in Pune so I am going to take the advice of this professor and visit the ashram. I expect I shall stay in Pune for a few hours and leave this evening.

Chapter Twelve
An Ashram in Pune

Monday, 28th June

I am still here in Pune because this is an amazing place. When I got off the train I took a rickshaw from the station to the ashram. I was very surprised to see many people dressed all in orange going in and out of the front gate – the men all have long hair and beards and many people including westerners, are wearing long orange robes. I saw many people hugging. Everybody wears a necklace of beads around their neck with a picture of the spiritual Master. I had expected that he would be living in a house alone or with just a few people and I thought I could go and have an interview with him and leave the same day, but it was not like that.

I went inside the gate and entered a small building which looked like an office on the left-hand side and said to the woman sitting there: "I want to see Osho★."

She said to me, "You will have to do three days of meditation first."

This was a blow to me. I had to make a decision then, whether to stay or go and so I asked if there were any cheap hotels nearby. She told me of one, but then introduced me to a woman who works in the ashram kitchen here, who in turn introduced me to some English people who have invited me to stay in their rented house by the river. They told me they would meet me after the evening meditation which is called Kundalini Meditation, and take me back home with them. The rent is cheap – including food, it is five rupees a day.

I went to look around the ashram which consists of three houses and their gardens. They are called Krishna house, Jesus House, and Lao Tzu House. Lao Tzu House is the smallest house where the Master lives in one room. Other people also have rooms in the house and in the other houses.

One place called Radha Hall, which is part of Krishna House, is used as a meditation hall. It has only three walls and looks out into the open air. Here I did Kundalini Meditation this afternoon to a background of torrential rain. There are four stages, all fifteen minutes: the first three are set to music. The first stage is shaking the whole body to loosen it up and get rid of all tensions; the second stage is dancing alone with eyes open or closed; the third stage is sitting down on the ground with eyes closed listening to beautiful music, and the fourth and last stage is lying down on one's back with eyes closed in silence. I love this meditation – it is good for both body and mind and is so relaxing.

After this, my new friends took me home with them in a rickshaw. The River House is very big. There are at present fourteen people living here, ten men and four women – all seem to be in their twenties or perhaps early thirties. I was taken upstairs to a kind of dormitory where mattresses are laid out. The people here all share the cooking and cleaning and shopping. Downstairs is the kitchen and a living room where many of the men play instruments at night and make music. The windows and doors open out onto the river bank where we can sit.

The atmosphere here is lovely but everything appears quite mad. All the people here in the house wear orange clothes all the time – they have become sannyasins, disciples of Osho – and they meditate every day and attend his morning discourses.

What kind of strange place have I come to?! In India you never know what kind of unusual adventure is going to happen next! However, I love all these wonderful adventures! Surely, in almost no other country in modern times would I find anything like this – disciples (western and Indian) dressed like monks living around a living spiritual Master as people did in ancient times!

Tuesday, 29th June 1976

I have been to one of Osho's morning discourses.

This morning I was woken up at six o'clock as the other people in the dormitory wanted to do Dynamic Meditation. They taught me how to do it. It is an hour long like all the meditations. There are five stages to it, all done standing up – first stage is chaotic breathing, second stage is catharsis (you can go completely mad, shouting and jumping, releasing all pent up emotions), third stage is jumping and shouting 'hoo', fourth stage is 'freezing' – standing quite still watching the body until the music starts, when the last – the fifth stage – dancing, begins. This meditation is amazing but quite exhausting. I have never done anything quite like it in my life! In these meditations we are not allowed to touch or disturb anybody else.

Afterwards I felt very refreshed and wide awake. I was then lent a bicycle and one of the other women in the house, who is also English but has taken the Sanskrit spiritual name of Veetrag, took me for breakfast to a cafe called Cafe Delight which is on the way to the ashram. From there we cycled to the front gate of the ashram, left our bicycles outside and went in.

Everybody was going into Lao Tzu House. Lao Tzu House also has its own gate and a winding path leading to a very large, round, white marble veranda which looks over the garden of many young trees. It has pillars around it and looks like a white temple that I saw once in a dream years ago. (In the dream I went into the temple and lay down on the floor in bliss, surrounded by white candles.) Here there are no candles but I love the peace and silence of the place. It is called Chuang Tzu Auditorium. (Chuang Tzu was an ancient Chinese Taoist Master, as was Lao Tzu.)

We sat cross-legged on the floor. There were a few people like me, not dressed in orange, but many people wore only orange clothes. I was wearing my black sari top and my long wrap-around skirt which has a cream-coloured tartan pattern on it. I have been wearing this all around India. There was a chair at the front of the auditorium and a door in the wall. After a while Osho came in and greeted everyone. He wears a long white robe and his hair is black, nearly turning white. He turned slowly, looking into all our eyes as he put his hands together in 'Namaste' – this is an Indian greeting with both palms together, as though in prayer.

He has such charisma and wonderful eyes. I was sitting a few rows from the front but he looked at me immediately, perhaps because I am new. Then he sat down and started speaking.

I studied Religion and Philosophy at college as my main subjects, and he used to be a Philosophy lecturer, a professor in an Indian university, but I have never heard a lecture like this before. The words were so beautiful, so meaningful, and spoken with such authority and love, that tears came to my eyes almost immediately.

He was talking about the Baul Mystics from northern India who are wild devotees of the Divine and who travel from place to place, village to village, dancing and singing their love for the Divine Spirit they call the Beloved. They have thousands of devotional songs that come straight from their hearts. They do not belong to any religion or tradition or creed. They celebrate life and this existence here now, and make no distinction between this world and the next. They believe that the Divine is everywhere around us and in everything. Everything is holy – whole – we are not to search for Heaven anywhere else, nor beyond death, but to discover it here now on this Earth.

Sitting here, listening to Osho speak, I felt the truth of these words – that this celebration and gratitude for life and this beautiful world is the only way to live; that Heaven and the present moment is a dimension that you can step into, and here I am stepping into it. Sitting here, it seemed to me that religion came alive for me as it never has before. I feel now that I am seeing the world for the first time, differently and positively through different eyes.

The thought came to me as we were all sitting there in spellbound silence – all of us who might be thought of as hippies and drop outs by some in the outside world – that this is what it must have been like in the times of Jesus. Followers gathered around Jesus in the same way and were not respected by the society and the religious leaders of the time.

I came out of the discourse in a dream. Osho's words rang with a truth I feel I have known all my life: that we really can step into Heaven in this life. I felt ecstatic and blissful and amazed. Today I talked to other people here and I have found out that many people came here by accident like me and love the discourses so much that they have prolonged their stay.

This afternoon I did Nadabrahma Meditation which is a humming meditation in three stages set to beautiful music and then silence. Later, at about four o'clock I did Kundalini Meditation again, which is my favourite meditation.

Afterwards I came home here to the River House, where I am now. I helped peel the vegetables and cook the dinner. Of course, we eat all vegetarian food here and the ashram restaurant also serves only vegetarian food. In it you can also buy tea and coffee, snacks and meals, but I will eat most of my meals here.

This evening some of the men are playing music again with various instruments – their music is spontaneous – and the rest of us are sitting around in meditation and drinking lemon grass tea. The lemon grass grows wild around the house. We pick it and put it into the tea pot!

I am longing for the discourse again tomorrow morning.

Friday, 2nd July 1976

What kind of madness am I in? I don't know. At the moment I am caught up in a whirlwind, so that I feel drunk. I am enraptured in a kind of bliss and happiness, full of apprehension and excitement. It is evening and again I am sitting on the floor of the downstairs room of the River House and people are playing music, while some have thrown off all their clothes because it is hot, and they are dancing. People dance by themselves in meditation.

Yesterday I went to the office and told them I have done three days of meditation, and to my delight the woman there booked me a Darshan for the evening. (Darshan is a word meaning 'meeting with the Master'.)

I was very excited all day. The evening before, the Scottish girl in our house helped me to dye my wrap-around skirt orange. I decided that I was going to wear an orange skirt and my black sari top. I was going to go in to see the Master half in orange and half in another colour! I decided I was also going to keep on my silver cross and chain that I have worn all around India – not for protection – but because I have been wearing it all the time on this trip.

In the morning I went to the discourse – it was as beautiful as ever. Still he is speaking on the Baul Mystics in this series of talks. At the beginning of the discourse, a sutra is read out. These are words taken from religious songs of the Bauls, I think. I have been told that each series of talks he gives is about different enlightened Mystics the world over. He has also spoken on Jesus.

I did some meditations during the day. There is another meditation that I love which is all dancing, called Nataraj: forty minutes of dancing with eyes closed to wild Indian music, then ten minutes of lying down in silence, flat on the floor, then another ten minutes of dancing.

I showered in the evening before going into Chuang Tzu to see Osho. He is allergic to smells and perfumes. I saw a woman sitting cross-legged on the roof of one of the houses (there are steps going up) and I went to ask her the time but she did not answer – she was deep in meditation. I should have realised!

When I came to the gate of Lao Tzu House some women sniffed me to make sure I had no perfume on me. Then I was allowed to go up the winding path to the round white veranda called Chuang Tzu with about twelve other people. As there are quite a lot of people here now, as many as fifteen people go in together every night to speak to Osho, but we can still speak with him individually one at a time.

There were two rows of us and I sat at the back. I could hear everything that was being said. People were asking questions and some were taking sannyas – receiving a necklace of beads called a mala and a spiritual name from Osho. Everything he was saying sounded so beautiful and so compassionate. He accepts every person just as they are. There was no judgement or condemnation in his words. He listens to what the person says and then responds. People were asking advice about personal issues. It seems to me that he sees beauty and godliness in every soul and helps them to see it for themselves – that is the main thing.

Suddenly unexpectedly, he looked across to me at the back and said, "What about you?" There were tears in my eyes which had started falling while I was walking up the winding path into the garden. The path reminded me of another recurring dream I used to have when I was at school, about a winding path leading to a secret garden where I loved to go.

I was called to sit in front of Osho by an Indian lady sitting next to his chair. She told him I am a teacher.

I don't feel that this is the right way to describe me really, as I have only taught in a primary school for one year.

I knew Osho was asking me whether I wanted to take sannyas and receive a necklace – a mala. I had already said 'no' to the woman who had asked me at the gate if I was going to take sannyas.

Immediately I told him that I did not understand what sannyas meant. Earlier, some woman I met outside who seemed fanatical had told me that she thought he was Christ or the Buddha come back. This upset me, so I said to Osho,

"I'm not sure exactly what it means. Wouldn't it be putting you before Christ?"

He was looking into my eyes. I wanted to look into his but they were so deep.

He said to me: "I understand. If you understand Christ, there is no problem. If you don't understand him, there will be problems." He continued, "To love Christ has nothing to do with being a Christian. It is a deep understanding of a certain state of consciousness. Christ is a state of consciousness, of silence, peace, bliss, of purity, innocence."

I feel that he is a great spiritual Teacher as Jesus was. I wanted to go on talking with him, so I asked, "If I accept you, am I accepting you as being the same? Is it not accepting one and rejecting the other?"

He replied: "There is no rejection in religious life. Religion knows no rejection. The very idea of rejection is non-religious. If you accept me, you have accepted all those who have ever walked on the Earth and have been religious – not only Christ, but Buddha and Krishna also. There is no conflict between Buddha, Christ and me. The conflict arises because of the churches and the organisations and the politics that go on in the name of religion. Then there is conflict and even the Christ of the Protestants is different from that of the Catholics."

Then, because I know that taking sannyas means that people wear orange like Hindu or Buddhist monks, I asked why we have to wear orange, and he replied with a twinkle in his eye, that it is because he is whimsical, eccentric about orange. It seemed to be a joke, and everybody laughed. I said that I would not know what to reply if people asked me about it and he said, "One does not have to explain everything in life. All that is deep is always unexplained."

I said I was afraid of making a commitment, afraid of breaking the promise, as I might want to get married in white. He told me: "I am not trying to dominate your future – not at all. I am not saying that in the future you have to wear orange." He continued, "Who knows what the future will hold. The future is not predictable. I am not talking about tomorrow. I say, be in orange now and the next moment will come out of it. Who knows what you may decide later on. There is no need to worry about it."

I felt that he could see into my soul. He said more which made it all seem very light-hearted and non-serious, just a game – I could receive this gift of a necklace now if I wanted it and it was just that, a gift for the moment. I decided that I would like to have it – I did not want to miss out if gifts were being given away! So I let him put the mala around my neck and then he gave me a spiritual Sanskrit name – Anand Devika – which he said has the same meaning as my birth name, Angela. He said: "Angela means angel, doesn't it? Devika also means angel – a goddess. Anand Devika means goddess of bliss."

He wrote my name with his pen on a piece of paper and signed it with his own signature in Hindi.

I then told him I have studied the subjects Religion and Philosophy at college and I asked him whether I should go back and finish the last year of my university degree course. He replied, "Yes, it is good to continue and finish it. It will be helpful. Philosophy cannot give much, but it can give you a framework. It can give you a certain language to understand things, a certain clarity about concepts."

I went back to my place in the second row clutching the paper with Osho's signature.

I sat there trying to hear what he was saying to other people, but I was so overwhelmed by what had just happened.

When I came out of the garden I saw the moon up above and people were standing around. The only way I can describe that moment was that it felt as though the moon's light with all its beauty had fallen all around me. I felt so much bliss.

I feel now that I am walking on a spiritual path – but I think I have always been – perhaps this is what I came to India for, just to acknowledge it.

Saturday, 3rd July 1976

Osho mentioned me in the discourse yesterday morning, after I had taken sannyas the evening before. He said, "Last night a young girl came to me who was very afraid. She said she was afraid to take sannyas because, she said, 'It would be putting you before Christ'." He did not say my name but he was looking at me over the rows of people.

This afternoon I started to sew myself a Tibetan robe. An American woman called Sushila who works in the kitchen has given me a robe but it is too big for me so I have taken it in. Also, I bought some orange cotton material and I have drawn around the Tibetan robe belonging to Ritambhara, the Scottish girl who lives in the house. It is a simple pattern and ties around the waist.

There is a sewing machine in the house which I can use. It is great fun to wear a robe. When I was in my teens I had a secret desire to be a nun which shocked and upset my mother. Now I can fulfil all these secret childhood desires in this lovely dream-like game! Many people wear robes here but some men wear only orange lunghis around their waists, or long pants.

I will go back to the ashram to do Kundalini Meditation later this afternoon. I'll stay in the evening for the music in Radha Hall which is played freely on instruments by the musicians – anybody can join in and play music on their own instruments, but the harmony and beauty of this spontaneous music is amazing. The rest of us can dance – everybody who is not playing instruments dances in the Hall. I love dancing. I have always thought that this is what religion should be like – with so much dancing and music and celebration. This is meditation as it should be – sincere but not serious. It is so joyful.

Wednesday, 7th July 1976

I am so happy here. Suddenly I have found a new freedom, a new joy in life. Now I can live in the present because the present is beautiful. There is a river outside which keeps on flowing. I want to be like this river and flow with life. For so long I have struggled to keep up with the world. For so long I have been trying to play a role – always rushing from one thing to another because I felt that I had to have a role, a part in society. I was a teacher. I had to be a certain person to fulfil other people's expectations of me at the expense of my own true self. I had to be an actor in the play of life. Now here I can stop acting. I can be myself. I can let go.

I love getting up early in the morning to go to the discourses – every one is so beautiful. I wish I had written about every discourse. I will try to recapture a few of the truths that Osho speaks about.

He gives talks on all religions and philosophies, and all the spiritual Masters the world has ever known. He tells us to 'surrender' to life in all its fullness and beauty in the present moment – not to be always chasing after the future. He teaches that as the divine is within each one of us, at our central core, we are therefore already perfect – but since early childhood we have been conditioned by society not to see good in ourselves but to see bad, and we have suppressed so many of our natural feelings like anger and sadness that we were made to believe are wrong. Suppressed feelings are not lost – they are released in other ways such as violence, or else they stay suppressed and people become nervous, neurotic and tense.

Here in the ashram, we are encouraged to be true to ourselves as individuals, to value ourselves and accept other people and life for what it is so that we can grow into more balanced and more joyful human beings.

Meditation helps us to become aware of the divinity around us in everything – animate and inanimate alike. Even a rock is the divine which has fallen asleep. Like the Baul Mystics, Osho teaches that godliness is everywhere and we only have to open our eyes and see it. God is not sitting somewhere in the sky, but is all around us, and within us. This very Earth (in its natural state) is 'the lotus paradise' and this very body (each one of us) is 'the Buddha' – meaning 'the awakened one'. How beautiful to see the world like this. To see the world like this is to wake up to a new way of being; to become conscious, to become enlightened, and to be respectful of everything in this wonderful universe.

So this is a lovely fairy-tale. I have become the disciple of a spiritual Master. It doesn't even matter whether it is real or not – what is reality and falsehood anyway? As Osho says and as Indian philosophy teaches – everything in life and in this world is like a dream anyway – 'samsara' in Sanskrit – as every event slips away into the past, and only the present moment is real. And I am in it now. I love to listen to him speak and learn this new way of looking at the universe as a divine place and a divine play. It makes me appreciate my life and this present moment.

Osho has a sense of humour which is beautiful. He tells jokes sprinkled amongst the words in his discourse. In the discourse the other morning (which was a question and answer session), the last question to be read out was this: "Why am I so crazy about you?" He answered, "Because I am crazy. Crazy people are always attracted to me. Crazy people are beautiful. They are the only sane people in the world." Everybody laughed.

In one discourse which I loved so much, Osho talked about the seven types of religion in the world. The lowest types are based on greed for Heaven and fear of hell – they are the religion of belief. Then there is the religion of the intellect, that of the scholars – mind-orientated – who study only the written word, become very knowledgeable but have no experience. The highest type of religion is that of the Mystics, based on intelligence, consciousness, meditation and bliss.

Tuesday, 13th July 1976

It was Gurupurnima day on the full moon; this is a festival celebrated all over India in July. On this day, Indians pay respect to their guru or spiritual Master, so many Indians came here for the day from all over India and the ashram was crowded. We had Kirtan – wonderful live Indian music and dancing, and lots of good food. There was an enormous celebration cake which was cut up into small pieces and everyone had a piece. Osho's father was walking around giving out sweets to everyone. He is a lovely old man in his sixties who lives with

Osho's mother here in the ashram. There has been a lovely festive atmosphere in the air for about three days, because two days before the actual day, preparations were underway and decorations were being made. We all had a Darshan with Osho in the evening with live music played by the musicians.

I feel that here I can have a lovely time with so much dance and music and celebration, and also live my ideals of vegetarianism and meditation and spiritual longing. Here I can have both worlds. Religion does not need to be serious and sad and I don't need to remain celibate. Osho is telling us not to repress our natural feelings and desires, but to live through them, to squeeze all the juice from life so that we live life to the full and nothing remains unfulfilled or unlived. He says that freedom of the individual is the highest value. We are free – but freedom means freedom for everybody, it does not mean that we should live irresponsibly or harm other people. We have to live as consciously as possible with awareness.

I have talked to some people who work inside the ashram. There are many types of work that people can do, including kitchen work and cooking, cleaning rooms and caretaking, gardening and construction work, typing Osho's discourses which are recorded, office work, photography, silk screen printing for Osho's book covers, and leading meditations and group therapies. When people have worked for a while and want to stay longer they are sometimes offered a room inside the ashram. There are not enough rooms for everybody though and many people rent rooms or bamboo huts outside.

Chapter Thirteen
Meditation and a Therapy Group

Saturday, 17th July 1976

I have just done a three-day therapy group called Intensive Enlightenment which I was advised to do by Osho. He gives this course to all newcomers. It was an amazing process.

In the ashram there are eastern and western techniques for spiritual growth. Meditation is an eastern method. There are many meditations that take place throughout the day in Radha Hall. Because modern man finds it difficult to sit silently, Osho has devised unique active meditations which release tension in the body and take us naturally into a state of stillness and silence. As well as Dynamic Meditation at sunrise and others I have mentioned later in the day, there is Gourishankar Meditation, the beautiful Prayer Meditation in the evening; Vipassana Meditation, which I did in Amsterdam; and Sufi Dancing which is almost like folk dancing in a circle set to beautiful devotional songs. Osho encourages us to experiment for ourselves and find the meditation techniques which suit us best as individuals.

The western techniques are the many therapy groups which people can take. They sound very exciting. Most of them have been introduced from the West by westerners who trained as therapists there. Psychotherapy is becoming popular, especially in America. The therapy groups involve techniques for human growth and consciousness. I was reading a book called *The Primal Scream* by Arthur Janov when I was in Amsterdam, and here in the ashram we have Primal Therapy to help people to resolve issues and dissolve traumas from their childhood. I think the participants also have to write a short autobiography so they can look at their life objectively. There are also Hypnotherapy, Vipassana, Tao, Tantra and Encounter groups (courses) which people can pay for and participate in if they want to.

However, Osho says that therapy groups are only a preparation for meditation, and meditation is the really important thing. He says that therapies can be helpful, especially for western people who need to be able to let go of repressed emotions and tensions in a supportive group setting. People really love the therapy groups. I think that Indians are more naturally able to go into meditation as it has been part of their culture for thousands of years.

I never knew that anything like these therapy groups existed anywhere. I think it is very exciting. I feel that I know nothing about myself and I want to learn. I would like to have the opportunity of exploring my own inner being. Osho says: 'love thyself' and Socrates has said that the most important thing is to 'know thyself'. Osho says that in order to love others, we have to learn to love ourselves first.

I think I have never really loved myself. We are usually taught by all the religions to deny ourselves. Because of this I have never really thought well of myself.

It was very exciting to do the Intensive Enlightenment group. It has just finished. It was residential and food was included. We slept on mattresses at the top of Krishna House on the roof where there is a mosquito net all around.

It was a very structured process. From morning until night we sat with a partner (changing partners every few minutes when the bell sounded) and asking each other, "Tell me who you are."

Each of us spoke for five minutes about ourselves and then we changed over. The other person was told to sit and listen in a mirror-like way making no comment and using no judgment. We exhausted the outer information about ourselves – our name, family, country and friends and then we found deeper insights: we started to talk about our feelings and emotions.

After a while I realised that personality seemed to be superficial – that perhaps these things I felt about myself are not really true – that there are deeper, more unconscious layers. We talked about our childhood – our experiences as we were growing up. I feel now that I have always somehow been acting a part and suppressing my real self.

We did Dynamic Meditation in the morning at six o'clock and Kundalini Meditation in the evening. We were not allowed to converse with the other participants at all in any other way so it was a very intense process and very tiring – it stretched us to our limits.

I have never talked about myself before so intimately to anybody, and I felt that I could go on talking forever. I have always thought of myself as stupid and weak. I found it wonderful that the other person should put so much trust in me by telling me about themselves. When the person looked into my eyes I felt immensely embarrassed at first. I felt that I was not worthy to be told all these personal secrets.

On the second day I uncovered some deeper layers of myself and I broke down in tears. I was embarrassed and I told the therapist in charge that I had better leave the group because I could not stop my tears. She took me aside and told me it was all right to cry, that previously I had been theorising about myself – asking and answering the question, and that this was not the way. She said that I had to go directly to my feelings in the present moment and learn to be in touch with my real feelings – not interpret them and put them through a sieve and sort them out as I have been doing all my life. She added: "There are a lot more tears where those came from."

After that I was able to go a lot deeper into my feelings and I felt that I was uncovering layer after layer of myself, digging deep and finding feelings that I had hidden and pushed down – feelings that were crying to be released. It was wonderful to see that everybody in the group seemed to be going through a similar process, that everybody had hang-ups and fears and emotions they have suppressed – none of us were alone in that. As time passed we all seemed to be able to let go more and more and go deeper and deeper.

Now that the three days have finished, I still feel that I have only just scraped the surface of my inner being. I feel that I really do not know anything about myself at all any more.

I have always been afraid that other people will not think well of me. In this process I have learned to feel more and more at ease with people and to feel more trust in the other than I have ever felt before; I can see how vulnerable everybody else also is and that we all have the same problems. I would like to participate in this group process again another time.

After the therapy group, we had group Darshan with Osho. We were sitting in front of him and he asked the group leader, Amida, how the group was. She told him that a song was playing in her head, so he said, "Sing it," and she did. I loved the song and so did everybody. This is what she sang:

*'I'm busy doing nothing,
Working the whole day through.
Trying to find lots of things not to do.
I'm busy going nowhere.
Isn't it just a crime?
I'd like to be unhappy,
But, I never do have the time.*

*I have to wake the sun up –
He's liable to sleep all day,
And inspect the rainbows,
So they'll be bright today.
I must rehearse the songbirds
To see that they sing on key.
Hustle, bustle,
And never a moment free.'*

Everybody laughed. I admired her spontaneity. Afterwards, we, the group participants – less than twenty of us – sat in front of Osho one by one and spoke about our experiences in the group. I told him that a lot had come up for me, especially about my childhood, and I said I could afford to participate in one more group, perhaps 'Encounter' or 'Hypnotherapy'. He suggested 'Hypnotherapy' – a softer group.

Monday, 19th July 1976

By now I should have left Pune and been on my way up the west coast of India to meet my bus in Delhi to return overland, but I don't want to leave here. Even though the monsoon rains have got worse, still I am enjoying it here so much. I have made so many new friends and I feel so close also to the people with whom I participated in the group therapy Intensive Enlightenment because we shared so much together. It is fun staying in the River House also. The water in the river has risen with the falling rain. In the evenings when it is not raining I sit on the river bank and meditate.

The morning discourses were in English until 10th July and then Osho started speaking in Hindi as there are so many Indian people also here. I do not go every day to hear them, but when I do it is like a meditation as I cannot understand the words and it is so peaceful and silent, sitting listening to him, and he looks into all our eyes as he speaks. The English and Hindi discourses are recorded and printed in books and sold in the bookshop here.

He says that in every age there are enlightened people on the Earth, and that there are many paths to the Divine – the closer we get, the more the paths at their heart become similar. He has talked much about Jesus and also about the gospel according to Saint Thomas who reputedly came to India. Not many people know about that gospel. He has talked much about Buddha whom he says is the greatest Master who has ever lived, and Zen which he says is the only living religion. He tells stories of ancient Zen Masters and Sufi Masters, of mystics and poets like Kabir, of devotees and singers like Meera, of saints like Saint Francis of Assissi, and sages like Zarathustra, and Mahavira of the Jain religion; also philosophers like Socrates. He loves Lao Tzu especially – the founder of Taoism who wrote The Tao Te Ching in ancient China.

The book, *My Way, The Way of the White Clouds*, which I saw in Amsterdam, is a book of the Tao. I love the teachings of Taoism which tell us to live in harmony with nature and to be at ease with ourselves, and, as I have written before, be like a white cloud floating wherever the wind takes us, in a let-go with life, rejoicing in freedom and living in gratitude, trusting in Existence and in whatever happens in this beautiful world. That is how I want to live my life. I think I wrote this in my diary when I was in Amsterdam, before I had even found this place. Then life becomes such a great adventure, such a relaxation and is a beautiful game.

There are only four of us women in the house, and two of the women have a boyfriend living with them here. I think they came here to Pune with their boyfriends. I have fallen a little bit in love with one of the men here who is about my age and is very good looking. His sannyas name is Shanti which means 'peace' in Sanskrit. He tells me he went to boarding school. I spend a lot of time with him when I am in the house.

Monday, 26th July 1976

I sat on the riverbank and wrote this poem:

> *The river flows,*
> *the river flows and floats,*
> *goes on forever –*
> *but time stands still*
> *and everything is moving*
> *round and round in endless circles.*

Tuesday, 27th July 1976

I am now feeling quite ill and I think I have got dysentery. In this season which is so damp, it is easy to get ill and two of the women in the house have got hepatitis. Their boyfriends are taking care of them. We do not have any fresh drinking water as tap water is not safe to drink. I usually drink boiled chai, or lemon grass tea all the time. Sometimes I have bottled drinks like lemonade. We wash up in the cold tap water though and perhaps that is why I have got dysentery. I might have got the dysentery through eating fruit or drinking the sugar cane or orange juice from carts in the street. It is poured into glasses that are often washed in dirty water in buckets under the table of the street barrows and stalls. It is so delicious though that I can't resist it.

I have not booked for the Hypnotherapy group because I feel so unwell.

Saturday, 31st July 1976

In the afternoon I was feeling ill and lying down on my mattress upstairs when suddenly the police came bursting in. I think no one else was in the house. I did not know why the police were there, but I was friendly to them and invited them in as I would have done in England, even though I was wearing only my nightdress! When they saw me at the door of the dormitory upstairs dressed like that, they were embarrassed and immediately turned to go down again, saying, "We are very sorry, Madam." They then left the house.

When I related the story to my house mates later they told me that the police were probably searching the houses rented by westerners in the area for illegal drugs as they think that all westerners come to India to obtain drugs, like marijuana. Some western travellers take drugs in Goa. The ashram is against drugs as they are harmful to the body and destructive for one's meditation. There is a notice outside the main gate saying that no illegal drugs or weapons of any kind are allowed inside.

Chapter Fourteen
Monsoon Floods and Inner Treasures

Sunday, 1st August 1976

The water in the river has flooded its banks! The river water came right into the house and flooded the living room and kitchen on the ground floor. Everybody had to help in rescuing things that were floating away – everything on the ground floor, including kitchen equipment such as saucepans and plates. All the cushions are soaked through and our clothes are wet as no washing dries in this weather. My dysentery is worse and I feel very weak. I hardly had energy to help rescue the things floating away. It is not possible to bail out the water as the river water is quite deep and we just have to wait for the water level to go down. We have to wade in and out of the house. It is not pleasant as the water is so dirty. This is horrific. Most of the time I lie on my mattress feeling ill as I don't have energy to get up.

Wednesday, 11th August 1976

Here I am lying on a hospital bed recovering from hepatitis! The name of the hospital is Jehangir Nursing Home. What a climax to my travels!

The last thing I remember is coming to this hospital for tests for dysentery with my friend, Veetrag, from the house. She has been such a good friend to me. I felt so ill that I begged the nurses to let me stay in the hospital so that I could get away from the damp house. However, they refused. Then when we came for the results of the tests a few days later, I collapsed and fainted at the reception desk so I was taken in after all. I cannot remember anything after that.

They tell me I was unconscious for three days, but apparently I was delirious and moving about and getting out of bed. I have no memory of it at all. They tell me I was a very difficult patient and apparently I locked myself in the bathroom and refused to come out, I shouted and screamed and spat all my pills out.

I must have been having a real catharsis in my unconscious state. The only inkling I have of it is that when I woke up on the third afternoon, I heard myself screaming at the top of my voice because I was being injected. I was being fed with an intravenous drip which I was trying desperately to pull out! I was very startled and embarrassed to hear my own voice screaming. I never would dare to do anything like that in my conscious state. I stopped myself immediately but I had no idea where I was at first!

Two of my River House friends and a nurse were standing by my bed. Everybody was smiling because I had woken up – nobody was angry at me for screaming or for trying to pull the drip out. The doctor told me that they thought I was going to die because I was so seriously ill with dysentery and hepatitis.

I looked up and saw that my friends had placed a picture of Osho over my bed. It was very comforting to look up and see it here. A deep peace came over me and is still with me. In the night I dreamt that one of my friends from the ashram was sitting at my bedside.

Since the day I woke up, I have been seeing rainbow colours like auras around everything. Everything looks so beautiful and the world looks magical and new. I feel so happy and joyful to be alive.

I know now that I nearly died. If this is what death is like, as blissful as this, I am not afraid of it at all. Perhaps I really died and have come back to life again!

Something wonderful happened on the afternoon that I woke up when I was alone. Suddenly I heard a voice outside of me speaking close up near my cheek. Very clearly and out loud I heard the voice say: *'I am with you.'*

I have no idea where the voice came from. Now I know that miracles are possible in this universe. How it happened I don't know, but I am so grateful.

The doctor told me that a telegram was sent to my parents saying that I was dying! Of course, I have sent another one now to say that I am all right. They must have been horrified!

Friday, 13th August 1976

The ashram doctor has brought me a gift from Osho – it is a beautiful little wooden box like a treasure chest with two of his hairs and his finger nails inside. He has sent me the message to place the box on my forehead when I am meditating.

I have had so many visitors from the ashram and Veetrag has been wonderful – she slept on the floor by my bed every night in the hospital when they thought I was dying, and now she visits me every day and brings fruit and runs errands for me. Many Indians sleep on the floor by their relatives in hospital here. I like the food in the hospital – it is very simple – mostly boiled vegetables and rice and dal (lentils) without spice. I am not allowed to have butter or cheese. The nurses are so gentle and kind. There are only a few beds in the ward – not many. I sometimes talk to the other patients, all Indian women.

I have lost so much weight that my legs are very thin and it has been difficult for me to walk to the bathroom. However, they are getting stronger now. I don't know how I managed it in my delirious state!

Saturday 14th August 1976

A funny incident happened a couple of days after I woke up from my unconscious state. A group of local Indian people from a nearby Christian church came and stood around my bed and started singing hymns. I asked them what it was about and the man who had brought them to visit another patient, replied, "You must turn back to Jesus. I saw the devil and all his angels standing around your bed."

It reminded me of a time when I was at college in Bristol and a woman from the Christian Union there told me they were praying for me because I had said I believed in other religions besides Christianity. They told me I was on my way to hell!

I started to laugh because I feel now as though I am in Heaven. What this man was saying is a lot of rubbish. However, I feel so happy that I cannot be angry about anything. To placate him I replied: "I have not turned away from Jesus. Osho is the same to me. I love both." I pointed to his picture over the bed.

The man seemed content with that reply. I suppose he became afraid when he saw me in my delirious state having my 'catharsis'. I feel so blissful and peaceful now and it must be because it released a lot of repressed emotions in me. I was not inhibited in any way because I was unconscious. Hepatitis has really seemed to trigger a very deep therapeutic inner process for me.

I am sitting up in bed drawing and colouring pictures in a book given to me by my friends. This is like a meditation for me, and the pictures look beautiful to me because of the rainbow colours I am seeing around everything! I feel very blissful, as though I have been through death and out the other side again, and touched the heights of Heaven in the process. Perhaps I had a 'near death experience' as they call it, but I can't really remember it. I have written and illustrated a poem about life and death being the same thing. It begins: 'Life and Death, you showed yourself to me; the same sweet lady with the beauteous face'.

I feel so much tranquillity. I am going to return to England to recover properly, because my body is still very weak, and also because my money is finished. I will go to college in the town of Bath and finish the last year of my degree course with Bristol University. The money I have brought here has all been spent on hospital bills, and I will have to be repatriated from India. I have contacted the British Consulate and they will lend me the money for the flight. I can pay back the money later.

Wednesday, 25th August 1976

I have so much to write about! I am now on the plane going back to England. Here I am sitting on the seat in my long cotton orange Tibetan robe that I made, still feeling weak from hepatitis but well enough to travel. I wonder if my attire looks strange to the other passengers! I know that my parents are meeting me at the other end.

I will continue the story from where I left off:

I stayed in the hospital for nearly three weeks altogether and somebody from the British Consulate visited me and arranged my flight home. I did not have quite enough money to pay for the hospital bill and even though the British Consulate had agreed to lend me the money, it did not arrive before I left, so my friend lent me the extra money I needed which I will pay back when I get home.

On the morning of the flight, I got out of the hospital bed early because I wanted to go to the morning discourse in the ashram for the last time, but the nurse came and told me I could not leave until the doctor signed me out. They had originally told me he would be there early, so I was all ready to leave but I was then informed that he was not coming until nine o'clock, too late for the discourse, so she said I couldn't go. This was unbearable for me, so I waited until she had left the room and then made a dash for it. I wanted so much to go to the discourse and hear Osho speak one more time before I left!

My legs were so weak that I could hardly walk but I managed to get up the road and hail a rickshaw. The nurse caught up with me and tried to stop me. I begged her to let me go, and promised I would return after the discourse to have the doctor sign me out. Finally she agreed.

The other nurse on duty commented, "I must go and see this man!"

I got to the discourse in time. I felt so much at peace with myself and with the world – so happy to be alive. I walked slowly up the little winding path through the garden to Chuang Tzu Auditorium in the early morning sun with such a quiet mind, gazing at the lovely plants growing all around me. The world looked so green and fresh and so beautiful in the monsoon light.

It seemed so long since I had been out in the world (since before my illness) and everything seemed extra heavenly as though there was a white light in the air which hung around us and over us from a different realm. The plants looked to me as though they were pointing towards the heavens in an act of worship. I cried throughout the whole discourse as I listened to Osho speak about Gautum the Buddha and his teachings on non-attachment.

Before I left Pune in the evening for the night flight, I was allowed to have a 'Leaving Speaking Darshan' with Osho. I sat in front of him in Chuang Tzu Auditorium and apologised for not being able to cross my legs as they were still too weak.

He asked me if I had received the small box that he sent in to me as a gift, and I said, "Yes."

I told him, "I feel so blissful," and he replied, "That is because you have been very close to death."

I realised then that he knew how ill I was. I told him about the 'voice' I heard in the hospital, and lastly I told him that I am going back to England. Seeing how weak I am, he replied, "It is good."

At the end, he asked me, "When are you coming back?" and I answered that I am not sure. Then he said, "You will come back."

I know I am weak and that I need to go back to gain strength, but I also know with my whole heart that I will come back to India again. There is no doubt about that!

Veetrag and another friend came with me on the train to see me off on the plane at Mumbai★ Airport. I was so weak that I could hardly carry my bag, even though it is very light. When we arrived at the airport, we were told that the plane was going to be delayed for a whole day! The airline put me up in a hotel for the night. It was a luxury hotel with a revolving restaurant at the top and was near to Mumbai beach! I have never stayed in such a luxurious hotel before!

My friends were allowed to stay with me in the room overnight and they shared my food. I ordered extra toast for us for breakfast, and coffee mid-morning. We had a lot of fun. In the morning we went for a walk on the beach and happened to pass though the foyer of the hotel next door and were spotted by an Indian film company making a film in that hotel. We were invited to be in the film! We happily agreed as we were told we would be paid for it. Our role in the film was very easy. We had to sit at the back of the restaurant at a table and drink milk-shakes while an Indian actress was singing! My friend had his wallet stolen on the train so the payment for this helped him. I also sold my sleeping bag in a shop in order to get some money back for him.

Finally this afternoon I boarded the plane, and am now on my way home!

Tuesday, 31st August 1976

I arrived in London wearing a thin orange robe and sandals because I did not have any warmer clothes. My parents were there to meet me and were shocked to see how I was dressed, but it was so wonderful to see them. I burst into tears, but it was through happiness!

How can I describe how I feel now after this wonderful trip, the end of something which feels like only a beginning? How can I describe in ordinary words, my feelings, my experiences of those months that I spent wandering, travelling and exploring? I would like to do this my whole life.

There are no words for it, no words to describe such an adventure – the journey of a lifetime. I felt at the end that if I had been fated to die as a payment for the trip and what I had gained, then it would have been worth it.

India has drawn me like a magnet since the age of eleven. I had always thought, 'Perhaps the magnet is drawing me towards my death' but I had to take the risk. I didn't care about the risk.

I felt safe when I was travelling – not because I believed that the Divine was protecting me. Why should I be protected rather than other people?! But because I felt that I could accept whatever happened to me; that whatever happened would be surely right, would be my destiny – the will of the Whole. I had trust in that, and I felt, 'what could I lose except my life, after all'? I very nearly did lose my life at the end of the trip when I got ill. Adventure always includes danger and risk.

To wander the Earth and go into the unknown is the greatest adventure of all, as hopefully it teaches us wisdom and understanding – for not only do you learn about this beautiful, magical, miraculous world and everything in it, embracing all, but also such an experience, especially that of travelling to India, takes you to the depths of your own being, to your innermost centre. It is both an outer journey and an inner journey. The inner journey takes one into meditation, into one's own soul. In India I have found my soul.

Notes

*Note: When this diary was written in 1976, Osho was then called Bhagwan by his disciples. This means in Sanskrit, 'one who has attained to God'. In the earlier years, while he was travelling all over India teaching, people had called him Acharya – which means 'spiritual teacher' and soon they started calling him Bhagwan.

In 1989 in Pune, he said he had become tired of being referred to as Bhagwan. He did not want to be called this anymore. The name Osho was mentioned to him and he liked it. This name Osho sounds like 'oceanic'. It originally comes from Japan and is sometimes used in the Buddhist tradition by disciples as an address for their enlightened Masters. He said he would like to be referred to by this name in future.

The books of Osho's discourses now published, bear the name Osho. When I originally wrote this travel diary, I used the name Bhagwan to refer to him, as people did at that time, but since he has asked in future to be referred to as Osho, I have changed the name in my diary to Osho.

Osho's birth name was Rajneesh Chandra Mohan and he was born to a Jaina family in a village in central India. He graduated from the University of Jabulpur with a first class honours degree in Philosophy, and worked as a professor of philosophy at several universities in India.

He became enlightened at the age of twenty-one in 1953 and travelled all over India conducting meditation camps and

Notes

giving talks to thousands of people. Finally in 1974, he settled in Pune, two years before I visited his ashram.

In 1989, before he left his body, Osho suggested that his ashram in Pune be renamed: 'Osho International Meditation Resort.' It is a place where people from all over the world can come and meditate.

*Note: The town of Pune was called Poona and the city of Mumbai was called Bombay at the time of writing this diary. I have updated the original spellings.

Acknowledgements

With thanks to Veena Schlegel and Savita Brandt for their useful suggestions and help with editing. Also I want to say thank you to them for their own wonderful books.